Probate Records and the Local Community

Edited by Philip Riden

ALAN SUTTON
1985

Alan Sutton Publishing Limited
Brunswick Road · Gloucester
First published 1985

British Library Cataloguing in Publication Data

Probate records and the local community.
 1. Probate records—England
 I. Riden, Philip
 942   DA25.Z5

ISBN 0-86299-106-4

Typesetting and origination by
Alan Sutton Publishing Limited.
Photoset Times 11/12
Printed in Great Britain.

Contents

Introduction

During the last twenty years or so, students of many aspects of early modern society have exploited the seemingly limitless potential of probate records, especially inventories, for shedding light on previously little known corners of English history. As the documents have become available in almost every diocese in England and Wales in vast quantity, in some cases with newly compiled indexes to places and occasionally occupations alongside the contemporary name-indexes and calendars, so it has become much easier to make extensive use of the material. The advent of cheap photocopying has further facilitated their use, perhaps especially by groups of amateur historians studying their own community in depth. At national level, the records of the two provincial courts have become more easily accessible in the Borthwick Institute at York and the Public Record Office respectively, and in the case of the Prerogative Court of Canterbury, it has finally become possible to make use of the inventories exhibited to the court as well as the register copy wills.[1]

As probate records in different parts of the country have been explored with more than merely genealogical ends in view, so more has been discovered and written about the documents themselves, as well as what can be learned from them. Numerous collections of inventories have been published, normally with an introduction describing the administrative process which created the material in the first place, and usually also with a glossary of technical or obsolete terms found in the documents.[2] On the other hand, despite the enormous use made of probate records in recent years, either in record publications or secondary work, there is still no general guide to the material. Thus anyone preparing an introduction to a new edition of inventories, or simply a lecture to undergraduates, trainee archivists, extramural students or whoever, must still draw together information from earlier editions or any general comments made by writers who have used the documents in studies of early modern economy and society. This lack of an overall study of probate records is the justification for publishing this collection of papers, originally presented at a conference organised by the extramural department of University College, Cardiff, at Gregynog, the University of Wales residential centre in Powys.[3]

All the essays here should be of interest to local historians seeking to make use of probate records in a study of their own community and should also have something of value for scholars with wider interests. Mr Moore's paper is wholly general (thus relieving the editor of any obligation to provide a similar account of the material in this introduction) and all the other contributions make some points of more than local interest, while at the same time emphasizing the value of probate records in local studies. The essays relate to several different parts of the country, to rural areas as well as towns, and make use of both wills and inventories. When probate records first became easily accessible there was a tendency for historians to concentrate almost exclusively on the information about farming, trade, industry and housing which could be drawn from inventories, and to neglect wills, considering them only of interest to genealogists. In fact, as most students of the material now recognise, one should look at all the documents put into court in connection with a grant of probate or administration, since both wills and inventories can be of value in different ways, and for very detailed local studies even the humble bonds drawn up for grants of administration can contain scraps of useful information. Three of the papers in this collection demonstrate how much can be learnt from wills as well as inventories. This is perhaps a point which should be borne in mind by anyone preparing an edition of probate material: a far more rounded picture will be presented of the men and women whose next of kin exhibited inventories to the court if an abstract of their will (where one was made) is printed alongside a transcript of the inventory.[4] Another general point which should be obvious from the papers printed here is the need to understand the administrative framework within which the documents were created. There is a temptation, not always resisted either by amateur local historians, graduate students or others who should know better, to seize on a large body of interesting and reasonably homogeneous material such as probate records, and to subject it to fairly elaborate analysis without taking account of the strengths and weaknesses of the source. None of the papers in this volume attempts to provide a full account of the working of the church probate courts but they should at least help anyone who in the future sets out to write such a study.

All the essays will, I hope, encourage further work on probate records in different parts of the country. Few if any of the topics considered here are by any means exhausted. It is possible that the publication of simple editions of transcribed wills and inventories for particular communities has now reached a stage at which diminishing returns are setting in, although one can argue that such volumes (or merely the preparation of unpublished transcripts of inventories) adds to the total quantity of material easily accessible for study and certainly relieves what are often fragile documents from further handling in record offices.[5] It is also true, as many local history societies and extramural tutors know, that local groups generally enjoy transcribing and publishing collections of inventories relating to one community, irrespective of any wider interest which the documents may have. On the other hand, few would deny that what is now needed, in addition to a study of the ecclesiastical probate courts, is more analysis of the documents besides mere transcription and publication.

The question of who made wills, or what proportion of the population came within the purview of the local or provincial courts has yet to be resolved, and can only be by painstaking local studies in which the frequency of probate grants is compared with burials in parish registers. Did attitudes to will-making change between, say, the sixteenth century and the mid-eighteenth, the period in which inventories are most numerous and probate records have been most widely exploited? How precise is the correlation, presumed to exist and assumed to be positive, between wealth and will-making? Who exactly, in a local community, dealt with the consistory court and who chose to prove their family's wills in one of the prerogative courts, even if the estate in question lay entirely within a single diocese? Looking at a later period, it may be of interest to investigate the impact of the Probate Act of 1857 which established a new lay court in place of the church courts. Did more people make wills after 1858 than before? These and many other questions about the mechanics of will-making and will-proving deserve further attention, not least through local studies of the material.

Another direction which future work on probate records might usefully take, as more than one student of the subject has suggested,

is the collection of inventories (and other documents) relating to
men and women of the same trade in different parts of the country.
This is very much easier in those dioceses where something has been
done towards making indexes of occupations, or where large
numbers of documents have been printed or transcribed. Elsewhere
it would involve the examination of vast quantities of inventories in
search of those relating to a particular trade. Work of this kind,
however, would obviously be highly rewarding. Some early modern
industries, for example the leather trades, seem to have left virtually
no records apart from inventories drawn up after the death of
craftsmen employed in them. Thus an overall view of tanning and
shoemaking in the sixteenth and seventeenth centuries will only
emerge from a widespread examination of probate records in search
of tanners and shoemakers, ubiquitous and in some districts very
important craftsmen who are otherwise virtually undocumented.[6]
Similarly, in the iron industry, about whose general history a great
deal is known, inventories can supply information about some of the
lesser figures in the trade to an extent that has probably still not
been fully realized. David Hey and Marie Rowlands have demonstrated the potential of inventories in bringing to life the secondary
metalworking trades of the Sheffield region and the West Midlands
respectively, but elsewhere there may well be inventories of ironmongers, nailmakers and small merchants to be found to provide a
fuller picture of exactly how the industry operated.[7]

Wholesale and retail distribution, as Dr Hey has more recently
shown and as Mr Vaisey's paper here demonstrates, is another little
explored branch of the early modern economy where wills and
inventories seem to be the only widely available source.[8] As each
new collection of urban inventories is published, so it becomes
clearer that sixteenth- and seventeenth-century townspeople were
more familiar with shops than was once believed, and that shops in
provincial towns stocked a remarkable variety of goods, many of
them imported.[9] But the process by which these goods reached
retailers, either from the ports or places of manufacture elsewhere
in Britain, has still to be fully worked out. Not only would the
comparative study of retailers of the same type from different towns
help but so also might a determined search for the probate records
of those engaged in the actual distribution of goods. Carriers,
chapman, badgers, swailers and other middlemen remain remarkably elusive individuals, although some of them must surely have

made wills.[10] Inventories of all kinds can supply odd snippets of information about the distributive mechanism in early modern England: a note that appraisers had disposed of part of the deceased's estate before probate establishes the continued existence of a fair in a nearby village; a list of Cardiff shop-stock said to have been bought at the last Bristol fair confirms the dominance of that city in the local economy of South Wales; or the appearance of Kendal, Rochdale and Shrewsbury men among the creditors of a Chesterfield draper illustrates the wide choice of cloth available in the latter place in the 1580s.[11] Perhaps one day it will be possible to link names found in lists of debtors and creditors in one part of the country with inventories belonging to those men in another and thus more will be discovered of the network of credit and internal trade beyond an immediate locality.

These suggestions only touch on the potential that still remains for the use of inventories in the study of the early modern economy, despite all the work that has been done in recent years. Other areas of enquiry have perhaps been more fully explored. Two, which remain very important but are not represented in this collection, are farming, for which inventories remain an unrivalled source, and (combined with fieldwork) vernacular building. The use of probate records for achitectural history, using inventories in which the contents of a house is itemized room-by-room, leads on to the analysis of how each room was furnished. Work of this kind has an obvious appeal where one can match inventories with surviving buildings and its results can be seen especially clearly in museums in which reconstructed houses have been furnished entirely in period. To go into one of the more prosperous farmhouses at, for example, the Welsh Folk Museum at St Fagans, is virtually to walk into an inventory from the Llandaff consistory court records. One way in which this work may possibly be developed is to use inventories as a rough measure of the growing material wealth of a large section of the population in the century or so before the Industrial Revolution. Sixteenth-century inventories have long been scoured for early references to window-glass or the first appearance of the 'parlour' as signs of increasing affluence, but the period 1660–1750 may also repay closer attention. Is it possible at least to identify, if not actually explain, the great increase in the consumption of iron in Britain in the later seventeenth century, much of it imported, by looking for a wider range of domestic ironware in inventories in this period, or was it the case by this date that appraisers no longer bothered to itemize every firedog, andiron and spit-hook with the care which their Tudor predecessors apparently did? The close study which very large numbers of Shropshire inventories are currently receiving suggests that some clues as to the growth of a consumer society may be gleaned from inventories after 1660.[12]

The value of inventories for architectural history, and for students of furniture, decoration and similar topics, may be particularly great in the case of those exhibited in the Prerogative Court of Canterbury, which attracted suitors of far greater standing than any local court. When the PCC inventories, now available after years of neglect, are fully examined by local historians all sorts of hitherto unimagined treasures may be unearthed. With local knowledge it should be possible to match a considerable number of inventories to identifiable, and in some cases surviving, buildings, perhaps especially the homes of 'parish gentry' or well-to-do merchants who tend not to leave family and estate papers but whose houses may still be standing and who normally had wills proved in PCC rather than locally. In the course of listing, a number of nationally famous individuals, houses and events were noted by the staff at the PRO among the PCC inventories. It may well be that similar discoveries at regional level now await the local historian who can visit London and examine the documents against a background knowledge of a particular part of the country. There are obviously far fewer PCC grants (and even fewer with surviving inventories) for any one town than can be found for the same place in the local probate court but the small quantity may be compensated for by the greater interest of each document.[13] It is a pity that, while the List & Index Society has done good work in reproducing PRO lists of the new PCC classes, the publication of nominal indexes to PCC grants, carried by the British Record Society to 1700, has now apparently defeated the Society of Genealogists, whose index for the period 1750–1800 is very far from completion.

None of the papers in this volume deals specifically with PCC records, although one hopes that before long the Public Record Office will themselves produce a handbook to this group, which is so heavily used both by genealogists and searchers with wider interests. A collection of only five essays inevitably has other omissions. Scottish and Irish testamentary law (and archival survival) differ so much from the English pattern that they have not been tackled here.

The lack of any paper dealing with Wales perhaps requires some explanation, since after the Act of Union (1536) probate in Wales was identical to the procedure in England, added to which the conference at which the papers were originally given was held in Wales. I myself gave a short talk on South Wales probate records at Gregynog on this occasion, intended mainly to draw attention to what seemed to me the potential of the material for Welsh local history and touching on some of the problems of using wills and inventories in Wales, compared with my experience in England. At the time (December 1979) several groups in Glamorgan, either under the auspices of the Cardiff extramural department or independently, were beginning to exploit the Llandaff consistory court material on lines similar to those followed over a longer period in many places in England. One group in particular was well advanced in an ambitious study of the upland Glamorgan parish of Llantrisant. The potential for detailed community studies centred on probate records thus seemed considerable and the problems less so. The unpublished nineteenth-century manuscript index to the Llandaff probate records had been photocopied and made available in Cardiff, while the National Library of Wales, at which all Welsh consistory and archdeaconry court records are kept, was able to supply xerox copies of documents cheaply and expeditiously. Three studies based on parishes in the Vale of Glamorgan, including the small town of Cowbridge, were actually completed by extramural classes and the results published by the department.[14] Students preparing dissertations for our local history diploma were able to acquire copies of inventories for communities on which they were working. Perhaps naively, I believed that future prospects for the study of early modern south-east Wales using this material (combined with what little else was available for any particular parish) were bright. Since then, the National Library, apparently alone among repositories that house original wills and inventories, has imposed what can only be interpreted as a penal charge for supplying xerox copies of such documents, currently £1.50 per grant, irrespective of the number of sheets to be copied. While a family historian seeking wills for a couple of ancestors will probably not be deterred by such a charge, an extramural department trying to organize a research class undoubtedly will. There is now little hope for any group (except perhaps a very wealthy local history society) seeking to tackle a detailed community study similar to those which classes were able to complete a few years ago. Problems have thus replaced potential in the use of probate records in South Wales and the lecture which I gave at Gregynog, points from which were in fact embodied in one of our department's publications, now seem sadly out of date.[15] For this reason I have not included it here.

Apart from this cloud, prospects for futher work on probate records for all kinds of local history remain good, whether it be a full-scale community study, an analysis of local building styles, the study of particular crafts, or more intractable topics such as internal trade or the growth of a consumer society. A great deal of work is currently in progress, new techniques of analysis are evolving, more collections of transcripts are being made available for wider study. The essays published here should suggest new lines of enquiry and provide comparative material for local historians in many parts of the country. They should also be of general interest in urging care in the use of the documents and in stressing the importance of understanding how wills and inventories came into existence in the first place.

The five papers have been printed here more or less as they were delivered at the conference, with a varying degree of informality of style retained. It should also be borne in mind that the references in general reflect the state of work on probate records in 1979, rather than now, although there remains no major study of the documents and their use by historians. Hence the justification for publishing this volume, albcit some time after the conference for which the papers were written took place.

Philip Riden
August 1984

Notes to Introduction

1 This introduction is intended to complement Mr Moore's general paper which follows; for this reason detailed references to standard textbooks and published editions given by him have been omitted from what is intended to be a more discursive treatment of the subject. Apart from my use of probate material among the records of the diocese of Llandaff, comments here are based chiefly on my experience of the Lichfield material for Chesterfield

(Derbys), some of which has been published by the Derbyshire Record Society *(Chesterfield wills and inventories, 1521–1603*, ed. J.M. Bestall and D.V. Fowkes, 1977), while the rest will be used extensively for my forthcoming Volume II of the History of Chesterfield being published by the Borough Council. I have also used PCC material for Chesterfield and hope that the Derbyshire Record Society will be able to publish an edition of local PCC inventories to demonstrate the exceptional interest of this material. My understanding of probate records in other parts of the country has been considerably enhanced by conversation with colleagues in the Association of Local History Tutors and elsewhere.

2   The only separately published glossary remains R. Milward, *A Glossary of Household, Farming and Trade Terms from Probate Inventories* (Derbyshire Record Society, 2nd ed. 1982).

3   Papers from a similar conference the previous year were published by the Cardiff extramural department as P. Riden (ed.), *The Medieval Town in Britain* (Cardiff, 1980).

4   As was done, for example, in the Chesterfield volume cited in n.1.

5   For a recent view of inventory publishing by an experienced editor see D.G. Vaisey in *Archives*, XIV (1979), pp. 108–9. The alternative view has been put to me by Mrs Nancy Cox, who has worked extensively on Shropshire inventories, that more transcripts, even if not fully published, are always useful.

6   The value of inventories for the study of the leather industry was first made apparent by L.A. Clarkson in 'The leather crafts of Tudor and Stuart England', *Agricultural History Review*, XIV (1968), pp. 25–37, or 'The organisation of the English leather industry in the late sixteenth and seventeenth centuries', *Economic History Review*, 2nd series, XIII (1960), pp. 245–56. All subsequent studies, including Dr Phillips's printed here, confirm this view.

7   D.Hey, *The Rural Metalworkers of the Sheffield Region* (Leicester, 1972); M. Rowlands, *Masters and Men in the West Midland Metalware Trades before the Industrial Revolution* (Manchester, 1975).

8   D. Hey, *Packmen, Carriers and Packhorse Roads. Trade and Communications in North Derbyshire and South Yorkshire* (Leicester, 1980), p. 9 surveys the neglect which this subject has suffered.

9   As well as Mr Vaisey's paper printed here, see *Yeomen and Colliers in Telford. Probate Inventories for Dawley, Lilleshall, Wellington and Wrockwardine, 1660–1750*, ed. B. Trinder and J. Cox (Chichester, 1980), pp. 20–41, a very detailed analysis of mercers' inventories from Telford and elsewhere.

10 The wills and inventories of several Chesterfield chapmen will be discussed in my forthcoming volume referred to in n. 1; carriers, including a 'London carrier', also appear in the town by the middle of the seventeenth century.

11 The first and third examples here are drawn from *Chesterfield Wills and Inventories;* several Cardiff inventories of the period 1660–1700 mention goods bought at Bristol.

12 Cf. n. 9; I am indebted to Barrie Trinder and to Dr and Mrs Cox for insights into their continuing work on Shropshire.

13 Cf. my comments about PCC material for Derbyshire in n. 1, where an

inventory has been found for Bess of Hardwick's otherwise undocumented prodigy house at Oldcotes.
14 M. Griffiths, *Penmark and Porthkerry: Families and Farms in the Seventeenth-Century Vale of Glamorgan* (1979); P. Riden, *Farming in Llanblethian, 1660–1750* (1980); Idem, *Cowbridge Trades and Tradesmen 1660–1750* (1981).
15 I.e. in *Farming in Llanblethian,* pp. 1–9.

PROBATE INVENTORIES – PROBLEMS AND PROSPECTS

John S. Moore

One of the inevitable problems in opening the batting on an occasion such as this is that I do not know either my audience or what my fellow speakers will be saying later. Consequently it is probable that much of what I will say may appear obvious or elementary in the light of later contributions and hence not very illuminating. Nevertheless, at the risk of setting myself up as an easy 'Aunt Sally', I think it is worthwhile looking at some of the general problems and prospects involved in using probate inventories before other speakers get down to the nitty-gritty of specific topics in specific places.

It is, I presume, common ground (otherwise none of us would be here this weekend) that probate inventories are important and valuable sources of information on many historical subjects, so I shall not waste time in saying what an inventory is – there are already many printed or typescript volumes of inventories available and more are known to be in preparation.[1] Later I shall mention some specific uses of inventories when considering 'Prospects', but I want to begin by examining the 'Problems'. Although each topic for which inventories are or could be used will have its own special problems and dangers of interpretation, there are also more general problems, arising from the nature and survival of the inventories we now have, which it is worth spelling-out in some detail.

To begin with, unlike the Scottish 'testaments', the English and Welsh probate inventories *only* deal with what the lawyers call 'moveable property', that is, goods and chattels, and leasehold interests in land. They do *not* deal with 'real property', that is, freehold or copyhold land, *nor* with what would later be termed 'landlord's fixtures and fittings.' A very important conclusion follows immediately from this limitation. This is that these inventories are *not* a reliable guide to the total wealth of any individual, nor can they be used for comparative analysis of relative wealth, unless it can be shown from other sources (such as manorial or estate surveys, rate-books or land-tax assessments) that the person concerned owned little or no land. Almost certainly the landed property owned by the aristocracy, gentry and most farmers greatly exceeded in value their moveable wealth, whilst the relative economic position of some middling social groups may be greatly altered by the inclusion of their landed wealth. Dr Margaret Spufford has pointed out that in the London Orphans' inventories she has studied there is not a high correlation between the ranking of values of goods and chattels and the ranking of total values including leasehold estates.[2]

Secondly, again unlike the Scottish 'testaments', the English and Welsh inventories give only the gross values of moveable estates. Unless either executors'/administrators' accounts or, in the 16th and earlier centuries, the lists of debts owed by a deceased person incorporated in his or her will, survive, it is impossible to calculate the net values of estates. This in turn presents further problems to historians: where probate accounts do survive (generally, rarely), it frequently appears that outstanding debts to others may severely reduce, and on occasion outweigh, the gross values given in the inventories. On the other hand, it is arguable that the amount of outstanding debt is an indication of the deceased's 'credit-rating' during his lifetime, and that, paradoxically though it may seem, his economic standing may be better measured by *adding* his outstanding debts to the gross value of his estate.[3] Whether or not this contention is valid does not seem to me to be of great moment, given the rarity of probate accounts or other sources of information on debts owed by the deceased. (Debts owed *to* the deceased are of course normally included in probate inventories.) Also, the economic standing of an individual will at least in part depend on his landed wealth (excluded from inventories as we have just seen) and on non-economic factors such as kinship and his or her position within the traditional structure of the local community.

Thirdly, apparent omissions may well be due to changing definitions of what constituted 'landlords' fixtures and fittings'. An obvious example here is window-glazing, which in my experience in

Gloucestershire is mentioned in pre-Civil War inventories but not in those of later date. We cannot deduce from this that glazed windows were rarer after 1660 than before, but rather the opposite: they had become so common that they were taken for granted as part of the structure of the freehold or copyhold building and therefore quite properly excluded from inventories after 1660. Their earlier appearance in inventories must hence be interpreted as meaning that, whilst glazing was rare, tenants who moved took their glass with them to their new residence.

Fourthly, regardless of the order in which the contents of rooms (where named) were listed, 'wearing apparell' and 'money in purse' come first in most inventories. This does not necessarily mean that the next room mentioned in the inventory is either the main bedroom or the main downstairs room of the house. It is also generally, and sadly, the case that clothing is rarely itemized, but nearly always included in the catch-all phrase 'wearing apparell'.

Fifthly, inventories nearly always omit food intended for family consumption: the foodstuffs that are mentioned are, I am certain, those produced for sale. Hence food of any sort rarely appears in the inventories of people, such as most town dwellers and landless countryfolk, who were only consumers, not producers. Furthermore, except in the inventories of bakers, I have very rarely encountered any mention of bread, which is known to have been a major article of consumption, or, except in the inventories of grocers, any mention of pepper, spices, tea, etc., though the frequent occurrence in domestic inventories of 'spice mortars' and the less frequent mention of receptacles for tea tell us that these were items generally found in most households. Again, this conclusion can be verified from other sources.[4]

In the sixth place, we must remember that executors and administrators were under no legal obligation to make inventories, or obtain probate, if the *bona notabilia* did not exceed £5. Generally speaking, I would think that relatively few inventories exist, certainly after 1660, having total values under £5. Even above the £5 level, there are numerous cases known to local historians all over England and Wales where not only inventories but also wills and administrations do not exist now, not because they have subsequently been lost but because they were never made at the time.[5] Either the property concerned had already been transferred before death, or informal arrangements were made after death which were concealed from the probate authorities. Both these factors have very significant consequences to which I will return. Also, we must remember that there was no legal compulsion on appraisers to name the rooms which were being inventoried. As a matter of convenience it was more commonly the case than not that rooms were named: in south Gloucestershire, for example, about two-thirds of inventories are listed room-by-room. But we cannot assume that the absence of room-headings means we are dealing with a one-room hovel.

Moreover, in dealing with what may be called the 'internal' characteristics of probate inventories, we must consider the values and totals. Taking the totals first, it is my impression that at least three-quarters of totals of individual values expressed in roman numerals are to greater or lesser degree inaccurate, and even those totals of values expressed in arabic numerals must first be checked. But a far greater problem arises in trying to decide what constitutes a value and verifying it. Fairly obviously clothing, most domestic furniture, utensils and equipment on farms or in workshops are being assigned a 'second-hand' value which may well be somewhat lower than their actual resale value; we simply do not know in most cases. But for crops, livestock, foodstuffs destined for the market, and metal goods valued on the basis of their price as scrap-metal, I am inclined to believe that their values closely and consistently reflect market-prices, since their 'second-hand' values are effectively the current values. Now clearly this is a hypothesis that may not be true nationally: certainly it needs to be tested in each market-region by comparing inventory unit-prices with prices from other sources, such as the accounts of estates, farms, households and institutions as well as 'assize of bread' and similar 'Grain Returns' price-series where available. This is a task I am attempting for the Bristol region, but I have not yet completed the collection of prices from inventories, let alone compared these prices with those from other sources. Nevertheless, I have already noticed that, for goods of consistent quality, the unit-prices used by different appraisers at different places within the Bristol region in the same year are generally fairly close to each other and quite frequently identical. Since there is no evidence whatsoever for collusion between appraisers within an area of 4–500 square miles, only one explanation is possible for this 'bunching' of prices, namely that the appraisers were genuinely basing their values on current market-prices within a coherent region dominated by the Bristol market.

And what, finally, of the awful possibility of deliberate omission? Precisely because of the irreplaceable nature of probate inventories, it is impossible to provide an external check on their contents except on the very rare occasion when in theory a non-probate inventory may have been compiled for the same person's property by a different authority. Such an eventuality is theoretically possible, but I have never yet experienced this conjunction myself, nor have I heard of any other student who has. A partial check may be possible where wills include detailed lists of specific bequests, all of which in theory ought to appear in the corresponding inventory: often, however, the items bequeathed may be subsumed under generalized phraseology in the inventory, so that this means of checking the inventory may in practice be ambivalent in its conclusions. We are therefore thrown back on internal checks, of which the most readily available is the detailed composition of houses in those inventories which list the rooms as inspected by the appraisers. Since upstairs rooms are usually described either as the 'chamber' or 'loft' or 'room' over a named downstairs room or as the 'Hall (or Kitchen or Parlour) Chamber', it is possible to detect when, apparently, a room has been omitted, e.g. if a Parlour Chamber is listed but not the Parlour itself. Nevertheless, even in this instance, we cannot safely conclude that the contents of the Parlour have been deliberately omitted: at worst only that the heading for the Parlour has been accidentally left out. But it is equally possible that the Parlour may have been empty, or the deceased may have let the room unfurnished to someone else. In neither case would there have been any need for the appraisers to mention the room since its contents, if any, were not liable to appraisal. An alternative approach is to compare the same house in successive inventories, especially if there are inventories for both a husband and his widow. Even in this case, discrepancies would not necessarily be the result of omissions: houses might have been extended: widows commonly converted their late husbands' assets into liquid cash for profitable moneylending: and, according to local inheritance customs, widows may have occupied only part of the family home or may have moved into a smaller house or cottage.[6] Internal checks will therefore not provide a reliable guide to possible omissions, but it is worth remembering that external checks were possible at the time that inventories were made, since creditors, executors, widows and heirs might all query the contents of inventories. But although disputed probate could give rise to numerous 'Testamentary' Cause Papers in the records of various ecclesiastical courts, such disputes are normally concerned with the non-payment of legacies or debts, or inadequate accounting by executors or administrators: it is fairly rare for inventories as such to be queried, which suggests that most were considered acceptably complete by well-qualified contemporaries. Moreover, as I have written elsewhere,

> 'in an age of which Peter Laslett has written
>> "all our ancestors were literal Christian believers, all of the time . . . their world was a Christian world and their religious activity was spontaneous, not forced on them from above",
>
> most appraisers would have had serious qualms about falsifying a document made under solemn oath. Without assuming that appraisers were infallibly accurate, we may nevertheless conclude that they were reasonably honest and conscientious, and that their work is worthy of serious consideration. Also, before we can convict them of error, we must be certain that our own conclusions are not based on our own unjustifiable assumptions – a case in point is the number of yeomen and husbandmen who die apparently leaving little money or household goods and no crops or livestock. Is it not more likely that the farmer has retired, allowing his son to take over the running of the farm, rather than that his neighbours and executors were either fools or knaves?'[7]

Let us now turn to consider the problems presented by the surviving corpus of probate inventories. An immediate question that arises is the size of that corpus, to which at present no answer can be given in the absence of lists and indexes for the major archival holdings. In many local archive repositories I would estimate that many tens of thousands exist among the diocesan probate series, and there must be about 70,000 in the P.C.C. inventories now being listed in the P.R.O. (PROB 4 alone contains about 30–35,000 inventories), whilst an incomplete sampling of the probate inventories at the Borthwick Institute in York suggests a total there alone of the order of 80–100,000 inventories. I would tentatively and conservatively consider the total of English and Welsh inventories to be well over one million: David Vaisey would put this even higher, at 2–3 millions. But the rarity of adequate lists, a result of inadequate levels of archival staffing, means that certainty about the total number of inventories and their chronological, geographical and occupational distribution is unattainable in the forseeable future, and without such a national list to act as a frame, true random sampling is impossible.

My own uncompleted sampling has already established that the chronological coverage of inventories varies considerably from diocese to diocese, though the period that is most commonly best represented is from *ca.* 1660 to *ca.*1720/30: that the period 1550–1660 is fairly well covered: whilst the periods before 1550 and after 1730 are least well documented. It is perhaps worth stating emphatically that the view that inventories originated with Henry VIII's acts regarding probate administration (21 Henry VIII, c.4–5) is indubitably wrong: these acts merely reiterated the need for inventories to be produced by executors and administrators. Numerous examples survive from the 15th and even the 14th centuries (some are in print) and these records are usually, but also inaccurately, considered to originate in Cardinal Ottobuono's Constitutions of 1268.[8] But these are only impressions of a general situation: in some areas inventories may not exist at all for the 16th century (e.g. Bristol deanery of Bristol diocese) or even for most of the 17th century (e.g. the Dorset archdeaconry of Bristol diocese): in most dioceses, inventory series die out during the 18th century, but in a handful of sees, they occur right down to 1857. Geographically, because of losses at sometime in the past, some counties have virtually no inventories from main diocesan probate series (Devon and Essex are cases in point), whilst the density of survival, even within the main periods covered also varies considerably from county to county, even within the same diocese: Durham has disproportionally more inventories than Northumberland, and W. Sussex (archdeaconry of Chichester) far more than E. Sussex (archdeaconry of Lewes). Sometimes, as in the volumes edited by Cash and Steer,[9] these deficiencies can be partly made good from inventories filed either among the records of Peculiars (areas exempt from the normal full diocesan jurisdiction) or among the Cause Papers of various ecclesiastical courts from deaneries or archdeaconries up to the Court of Arches or the High Court of Delegates, where these have been listed.[10] Since jurisdiction in disputed probate cases remained a matter for ecclesiastical courts until 1858, the Cause Papers in particular often yield inventories after the mid-18th century when most main probate series are rapidly becoming attenuated.

It is also clear from the volumes of inventories already in print that for any given area the occupational and social distribution of surviving inventories is quite severely 'skewed'. i.e. the upper and middle classes are over-represented (even more so if P.C.C. or York Exchequer and Prerogative series have been laid under consideration) whilst the lower orders are radically under-represented. The latter feature is, as I have already pointed out, perfectly explicable in view of the £5 limit below which inventories were not legally required, whilst the interest of local ecclesiastical officials in probate fees doubtless explains the greater concentration of inventories for the 'better sort of people'. Hence, in one area of south Gloucestershire, even one with an atypical degree of early rural industrialization, the gentry, professions and farmers account for 58.5% of all inventories, whilst agricultural labourers provide only 3.4% of all inventories,[11] though the local population as a whole consisted of about 10% gentry and professionals, about 25% farmers and 15% labourers, the remaining 50% being craftsmen, shopkeepers and artisans to whom about a third of the surviving inventories relate.[12] Clearly any selection of samples from such a collection must be 'weighted' to correct the biassed nature of the existing records where possible, though for many social groups the number of inventories is so small that the margin of error becomes very large. When only 4 inventories survive over 250 years giving the rooms in labourers' cottages in the Frampton Cotterell district, it is clearly unsafe to conclude that, since 3 cottages had 3 rooms and 1 had 4 rooms, the typical labourer's cottage contained 3 or 4 rooms, even though such a conclusion is *in the light of other evidence,* highly probable.[13] If necessary, we must *either* rely on the other evidence *or* cast our net further afield to secure a large enough sample of labourers' inventories to be statistically usable.

In part, it is likely that some of the non-random distributions, both geographical and occupational that I have mentioned, result from the process of compiling and keeping inventories. It is worth noting that some courts with probate jurisdiction retained the original inventories whilst others filed fair copies: in the latter case, there is the further likelihood of copying errors both in figures and in spelling, particularly if the probate clerks were unfamiliar with local dialect peculiarities. But a major problem arises concerning the increasing tendency in the course of the 18th century for the number of detailed inventories retained in probate collections to decline to a very low level or to be replaced by a short summary and total value. This tendency is so common in nearly all dioceses that it must represent a radical change in probate administration: either inventories were no longer being required from executors and administrators, at any rate in the old fully itemized format, or, if they were still being required, they were no longer being retained in probate archives. The first of these possibilities is in my view *a priori* unlikely before the 19th century: administration bonds, for example, continued to require administrators to exhibit inventories down to the 19th century, and occasionally both the full and the summary versions of an inventory survive to show that the latter was based on the former.[14] Certainly inventories continued to be made, and when specimens are available, either as exceptions in the normal probate series after *ca.* 1750 or in cases of disputed probate amongst Cause Papers, there is nothing to suggest that the appearance of an inventory as such was in any way abnormal. There are three further pointers in the same direction. In the first place, many diocesan record series include probate act books and administration registers giving the values of decedents' estates (which presumably must have come from inventories). Secondly, where the working records of local solicitors specializing in probate business have been deposited in local record offices, inventories are invariably present on the files of each client in the 19th century, as, indeed, they are to this day under the name of 'Valuations for probate'.[15] Thirdly, it is frequently the case that the probate records of 'peculiars' continue to preserve inventories much later than main archdiaconal or consistory probate series.

If, then, inventories continued to be made throughout the 18th and 19th centuries, only one explanation is possible for their non-existence in main probate series, namely the abandonment by clerks in probate registries of the practice of retaining originals or filing copies. Why this should be so I am not yet sure. Given the decentralized and lackadaisical administration of the latitudinarian Church of England in the 18th century, I do not believe that this change in practice arose out of any direction from the centre, particularly as the date of this presumed change in practice occurs at different times in different dioceses. Equally, I do not believe that it arose out of any recommendation for change in legal manuals, though this hypothesis may be more plausible if some registrars acquired new editions later than others: it is a possibility worth further investigation.[16] Tentatively I would suggest a more pragmatic reason, one which modern archivists and administrators should readily appreciate. This is that available storage space must have come under increasing pressure as a result of both rising population and the increasing length of wills which were being inflated by legal verbiage as their making came more into the hands of professional lawyers. In such circumstances, since wills had to be retained for possible later consultation (second grants of probate are quite common and even third grants are not unknown if executors died before winding-up estates or if long minorities were involved), it would be a natural reaction to abandon keeping inventories since there would be far less need to consult the latter once these had been exhibited in court and probate fees had been paid. And as not all probate registries would reach near-saturation point simultaneously, this would explain why inventories apparently fade out at different times during the 18th century.[17]

Another factor which would also influence the number of inventories made would be the degree of efficency of diocesan administrators, a factor that would clearly vary in different dioceses. In the diocese of Salisbury until the later 18th century, visitation articles required returns to be made of people who had died since the last visitation, of their executors and administrators, and whether or not inventories had been exhibited.[18] Such a regular inquiry would clearly increase the numbers of inventories made in Wiltshire, and it would be most interesting to learn if similar returns were made at visitation in other dioceses. The late survival of inventories in 'peculiars' would also point in the same direction: this could be explained partly because there was less likelihood of pressure on storage facilities but partly also because local officials operating within a small area of jurisdiction were far better placed to ensure that probate was applied for on death and to insist that inventories were supplied when required.[19]

Two final problems associated with inventories are worth mentioning. The first concerns editing and publication. Whilst I would maintain that the original spelling in inventories should be retained (for reasons I will discuss later), it does seem to me to be an unnecessary waste of space in times of high publishing costs to retain the original arrangement of inventories in columns, whereas a paragraphed arrangement under room-headings where given or otherwise under convenient topical divisions enables a considerable saving in space and therefore cost. Likewise, the repetitious reproduction of the standard heading 'A true and perfect inventory . . .' and the standard line openings 'Imprimis' and 'Item' seem to me a totally unnecessary extravagance, since all these can be omitted without loss and with a further saving of space and printing costs. Moreover, most volumes of inventories produced up to now have appeared as a result of commendable local interest and research, but in a totally unco-ordinated manner. I wonder whether there is not a case to be made for two alternative approaches: *either* a co-ordinated multi-volume edition of all the inventories for a few coherent regional areas *or* much more selective editions, designed deliberately to counterbalance the skewed occupational distribution of existing inventories by concentrating on the shopkeepers, craftsmen, artisans and labourers who are least well represented in local volumes.[20]

The second problem relates to the general question of using inventories for nation-wide comparisons, namely the evolution of satisfactory methods for producing standardized summaries and for preparing inventories for computerization. I do not pretend to be knowledgeable on computer methods, nor will I emphasize my lack of expertise in the presence of others much more qualified in this field. So far as standardized summaries go, I believe these are useful, indeed essential for some statistical purposes,[21] but that very often the exceptional detail or oddity, necessarily omitted in such summaries, can be as illuminating as the mass of figures. By all means let us count so long as what we are counting is worth counting: but let's not assume, as so many quantitative and econometric historians seem to, that only what can be counted is worthy of study.

You may think that I have spent an undue amount of time on the problems, but this is a necessary antidote to the euphoria so often induced by the very quality and utility of these invaluable documents. What of the 'Prospects'? I have already suggested that a major task must be the preparation of national chronological and geographical lists and of indexes by person, place and occupation/status. Without such lists, national sampling is hardly possible since there is no sampling frame. We cannot reasonably expect this to be done by already overworked record office staffs.[22] Either teams of researchers at county level must be recruited and their work co-ordinated, or a national team must be assembled with outside funding from a foundation or possibly the E.S.R.C. A preliminary task, on which I myself have been working intermittently for some years, is to discover from existing lists or by sampling where lists do not exist the main periods for which inventories exist in each diocese and the approximate number of inventories in each series. But the benefits to historical scholarship from a nationwide listing would be enormous, given the value of these records for so many aspects of the period from the late 15th to the later 18th centuries. Equally, further thought needs to be given to the problems of standard summaries and computerization as a pre-requisite to historical comparison and analysis: it is clearly neither feasible nor desirable to print every inventory, but it is both feasible and desirable to have available the essentials in a standard form.

The second major prospect, and a very necessary one given the patchy survival of probate inventories in both time and space, is to supplement probate inventories by laying under contribution inventory-type documents compiled for secular purposes. Parochial archives (now due for transfer to local record offices under the recent 'Parish Registers and Records Measure') incorporating detailed poor-law records may contain some inventories of paupers' goods compiled by overseers of the poor: these are rare documents but, where they exist, do throw light on the possessions of the social group least well represented in probate inventories. Many county record offices may have among the quarter sessions records inventories of the goods of insolvent debtors and bankrupts and such documents can also be found in some solicitors' collections: these, unlike the probate inventories, will include real estate (if any) as well as moveable property. Any inventories among municipal Courts of Orphans records should also be examined.[23]

But undoubtedly the major source of secular inventories is the Public Record Office, for a variety of reasons. Civil actions for debt gave rise to two large series of 'Extents for Debts' from 1320 to 1649 (C. 131, 239), continued by 'Extents and Inquisitions' (E. 143), a series running from the 13th to the 19th century, and in particular by 'Extents of Crown Debtors' (E. 144) from 1685 to 1842. This last series is especially valuable because it did not relate just to persons actually owing money to the Crown: the Court of Exchequer encouraged the development of a legal fiction, the procedure known as *quominus,* based on a fictitious allegation that A, because of a debt owed to him by B, was therefore the less able to pay his own (mythical) debt to the Crown. For brewers, innkeepers etc. 'Excise Extents' for the period 1760–1820 (E. 145) are also worth perusing. Debts owed could also be enforced by the use of 'minor' or 'procedural' outlawry, giving rise to two series (E. 172, 173) of 'Extents of Outlaws' running from the reign of Charles I to that of Victoria. Forfeiture of goods was also one of the consequences of detected felony, and several sources on occasion provide lists of the goods of felons: the medieval 'Escheators' Files' (E. 153); the medieval and early modern 'Escheators' Accounts' (E. 136, 357), 'Sheriffs' Accounts' (E. 199, 379) and the 'Extents and Inquisitions' (E. 143) already mentioned; the 'Special Commissions' (E. 178) from the 16th to the 19th centuries; the 'Inventories of Delinquents' (SP. 28/217) for the period of the Protectorate. The multifarious activities of the Court of Chancery from the 13th century on have given rise to Chancery 'Proceedings' (C. 1–3, 5–13), 'Masters' Exhibits' (C. 103–14) and 'Masters' Documents' (C. 117–26) all of which contain some quasi-inventories. Finally the Court of Bankruptcy 'Registers' Files' and 'Books' (B. 3–8) available from 1710 also include schedules of bankrupts' effects which, like most of the 'secular' non-probate inventories, do cover any real property involved.[24] It is also possible that inventories may be found among the depositions of Star Chamber (STA.CHA. 1–9) and the Court of Requests (REQ. 1–2) in the 16th and 17th centuries, and possibly among the proceedings on debt cases before sheriffs' courts in WARDS 9. Other outlawry series (E. 18/9–10; KB. 17/1; CP. 38/1–5) do not, however, include any inventories. Largely outside record offices as yet are another valuable source from the 18th century onwards, especially for farms, shops, mills and factories, namely fire insurance policy registers.[25] To what extent all the above-mentioned 'secular' inventories will make good deficiencies in the distribution of probate inventories will only become clear when the former have also been properly listed, but certainly the addition to the total corpus will be quite considerable.

I do not propose to speak in detail about the obvious prospects of using inventories to study the history of agriculture, housing, industry, domestic trade and the distribution of wealth in the early modern period. In these fields the utility of inventories has long been known and exploited.[26] It is, however, perhaps worth saying that the evident value of inventories should not blind us to the necessity of supplementing them with information from other sources: estate surveys and farm accounts for agriculture; surveys and sale particulars for housing; business accounts for industry and trade; whilst historians too often in the early modern period overlook the importance of archaeological evidence.[27] But I should like to conclude by pointing out some aspects of history where the evidence of inventories has not yet been fully exploited.

Although it is true that inventories generally cover clothing with the catch-all phrase 'wearing apparell', the exceptions to this rule are of vital importance, since these provide us with the bulk of our information on the dress of the middle and lower social groups. Up to now, the history of dress consists mostly of 'histories of costume', a concept of dubious value for social as opposed to aesthetic history.[28] In extending studies of literacy beyond the starting date of the Anglican marriage registers in 1754, inventories with the signatures or marks of their appraisers have a useful contribution to make provided that, firstly, 'weighting' is introduced to counteract their socio-economic bias, and, secondly, that their evidence is combined with that from other sources such as wills, administration bonds, marriage licences and bonds etc. With caution, it should be possible to determine on a regional basis the extent of literacy (as determined by the relative proportions of marks and signatures) from the mid-16th to the mid-18th centuries.[29] As I have already pointed out elsewhere, the network of credit-relationships revealed by mentions of debts in inventories helps to expand our knowledge of the extent of regional communities, since in the early modern period few local lenders would be so rash as to lend to borrowers whom they did not themselves know or who were not known to their friends and relatives.[30]

Lastly, a matter on which I have seen no previous comment in print, the study of local dialects. Most studies of local dialects are based either on 19th-century studies, especially those carried out by the English Dialect Society, or the Orton-Dieth Survey of English Dialects recently completed:[31] there are relatively few dialect sources in the medieval and early modern periods. But even in the 19th century local dialects were being assaulted by schoolmasters, the clergy and other purveyors of pseudo-gentility, and earlier, less contaminated source material is clearly needed. This requirement can be met by consulting probate inventories, documents compiled by local people who preserved phonetically both their pronunciation (sometimes a source of feeble amusement to the ignorant who have confused misspelling of a (wrongly) presumed standard English with a genuine attempt to render local speech in a recognizable form) and specifically local terms. In south Gloucestershire, for example, my *Goods and Chattels of Our Forefathers* traces back to the 16th century such common local words as 'wonts' (= moles) and such common local usages as the opening-up of dipthongs into disyllables, hence 'chair' became in script, as in speech, 'chayer'. I am sure that similar discoveries wait to be made all over England and Wales, and in Wales there is the allied question of the survival and evolution of Welsh as a vernacular tongue. I have, for example, noticed, in the course of my survey of Welsh probate series, that at least one Welsh diocese had some inventories written in Welsh, and I was informed by a Welsh-speaking member of the National Library staff that some of the words did not apparently survive in modern Welsh. In this as in many other fields, inventories not only present considerable 'Problems', but also offer enormous 'Prospects' to all historians.

Notes

1   A fairly complete list is available up to 1968 in M.A. Havinden, 'Household and Farm Inventories in Oxfordshire, 1550–1590' *(Oxfordshire Record Society,* vol. 44, 1965) and D. G. Vaisey, 'Probate Inventories of Lichfield and District, 1568–1680' *(Staffordshire Record Society,* Fourth Series, vol. 5, 1969). Later works known to me include J.S. Roper, *Dudley Probate Inventories, 1544–1603* (Dudley, 1965); M. Cash 'Devon Inventories of the Sixteenth and Seventeenth Centuries', *(Devon and Cornwall Record Society,* New Series, vol. 11, 1966); J.S. Roper, *Dudley Probate Inventories, 1605–85* (Dudley, 1966); A. Dyer, 'Probate Inventories of Worcester Tradesmen, 1545–1614' *(Worcestershire Historical Society,* New Series, vol. 5, 1967); P.C.D. Brears, 'Yorkshire Probate Inventories, 1542–1689' *(Yorkshire Archaeological Society, Record Series,* vol. 124, 1972); J.S. Moore, *The Goods and Chattels of Our Forefathers: Frampton Cotterell and District Probate Inventories, 1539–1804* (Chichester, 1976); E.R.C. Brinkworth, J.S.W. Gibson, 'Banbury Wills and Inventories, 1591–1650' *(Banbury History Society,* vols. 13–14, 1976); R.Machin, *Probate Inventories and Manorial Excepts of Chetnole, Leigh and Yetminster* (Bristol, 1976) and J.M. Bestall, D.V. Fowkes, 'Chesterfield Wills and Inventories, 1521–1603' *(Derbyshire Record Society,* vol. 1, 1977), but I

suspect that many more typescript volumes have appeared locally which have not entered the standard national bibliographies. I should be grateful for details of such works and of any now in preparation.

2 M. Spufford, *Small Books and Pleasant Histories* (1981), Table 1.

3 This point was forcefully argued in discussion by Dr Colin Phillips.

4 E.H. Phelps-Brown, S.V. Hopkins, 'Seven Centuries of the Prices of Consumables, compared with Builders' Wage-rates' (*Economica*, New Series, vol. 23 (1956), pp. 297–8); J. Burnett, *A History of the Cost of Living* (1969), pp. 30, 43, 120, 125–6, 129, 135–6, 138–9, 206, 273.

5 J.S.W. Gibson, *Wills and where to find them* (Chichester, 1974), pp.xv–xvi.

6 This factor is particularly well displayed in R. Machin, *Probate Inventories and Manorial Excepts of Chetnole, Leigh and Yetminster* (Bristol, 1976).

7 J.S. Moore, *op. cit,* p. 4; the passage quoted is from P. Laslett, *The World We Have Lost* (2nd ed. 1971), p. 74.

8 The view that inventories originated in the 1529 legislation is unfortunately given wide currency in an otherwise excellent introduction to historical source-materials: J.J. Bagley, *Historical Interpretation: Sources of English History, vol. 2: 1540 to the present day* (1971), p. 38. The earliest ordinance regarding the making of probate inventories appears to be one of the statutes for Bath and Wells diocese *ca.* 1258 requiring a 'scriptura que inventarium appellatur' (F.M. Powicke, C.R. Cheney (ed), *Councils and Synods with other documents relating to the English Church*, vol. 2 (1968), pp. 612, 618); in 1258–9 similar canons were promulgated by Archbishop Godfrey Ludham of York and Bishop Robert de Chariy of Carlisle for the northern province (*ibid.*, pp. 626–8, 658–9; M.M. Sheehan, *The Will in Medieval England from the Conversion of the Anglo-Saxons to the end of the thirteenth century* (Toronto, 1963), p. 213); and in 1261 the twentieth canon of the Council of Lambeth required the production of a 'de bonis defuncti fidele inventarium' as part of the probate process (Powicke & Cheney, *op. cit.*, pp. 681–2), at least for the province of Canterbury if not the whole English church (*ibid.*, pp. 660–1). The fourteenth Legatine Constitution of Cardinal Ottobuono, 'De executione testamentorum' (*ibid.*, pp. 764–5), therefore only reinforced existing legislation for the provinces of Canterbury and York. Sheehan (*op. cit.*, pp. 212–3) also points out that the making of inventories for deceased clerics had been standard practice since the fourth century; that there is at least one reference to an inventory being made for a layman in the twelfth century where the context does not suggest that this was abnormal; and that Magna Carta, c.26, had enjoined the making of inventories in administering the estates of deceased tenants-in-chief.

9 M. Cash, 'Devon Inventories of the Sixteenth and Seventeenth Centuries' (*Devon and Cornwall Record Society*, New Series, vol. 11, (1966); F.W. Steer, *Farm and Cottage Inventories of Mid-Essex, 1635–1749* (Chelmsford, 1950; Chichester, repr. 1969).

10 E.g. J. Houston, *Index of Cases in the Records of the Court of Arches at Lambeth Palace Library, 1660–1913* (British Record Society, 1972); K.M. Longley, *Ecclesiastical Cause Papers at York: Dean and Chapter's Court, 1350–1843* (York, 1980); 'Prerogative Court of Canterbury: Cause Papers, Early Series, 1642–1722' (*List and Index Society*, vol. 161). TS or MS lists of

other series of York cause papers exist at the Borthwick Institute of Historical Research, and for the Gloucester Consistory Court at the Gloucestershire Record Office, Gloucester.

11 J.S. Moore, *op. cit,* pp. 20–1.

12 *Ibid,* pp. 12, 15–7.

13 *Ibid,* p. 36.

14 *Ibid.* p.3, n.1.

15 E.g. Shakespeare's Birthplace Library, Stratford on Avon, ER 5/1–1100, (the working files of a 19th century Stratford solicitor with a large probate practice), contains inventories between 1802 and 1890.

16 But all the earlier editions of the standard textbook on ecclesiastical administration, R. Burn's, *Ecclesiastical Law,* still treat the production of inventories as a regular and necessary part of the process of obtaining probates. In the 9th edition of 1842, however, the editor, R. Phillimore, commented (Vol. IV, pp. 404, 421): 'According to the old practice of the Prerogative Court of Canterbury, an inventory was required to be exhibited before probate, but this has fallen into desuetude. . . . It is a matter of duty in the executor and administrator to deliver an account and inventory when properly called upon for that purpose; and in order to exonerate himself from liability, it is always most prudent to exhibit it before a final settlement. . . . An inventory exhibited before administration . . . is now fallen into desuetude, and according to modern practice is not exhibited. . . .'

17 This pressure on storage space would also explain why in some series (e.g. the York Exchequer and Prerogative probate series between 1591 and 1688, an example I owe to Dr W.J. Sheils of the Borthwick Institute of Historical Research, York) inventories have been 'weeded out' from wills and administrations and destroyed.

18 I am grateful to my friend Mr S.P. Gill of the Dept. of Theology, University of Bristol, for pointing out this important fact. *Cp.* P. Stewart, *Diocese of Salisbury: Guide to the Records* . . . (Trowbridge, 1973), pp. 45–7, 60, 66, 91.

19 This valuable suggestion I again owe to Dr W.J. Shiels.

20 The second course was vigorously propounded in discussion by David Vaisey; the point was also made that more volumes of urban inventories are needed to complement those for Chesterfield and Lichfield. The Avon Local History Association is considering the publication of a series of volumes covering the whole Bristol region.

21 One proposed standard form, developed by Mr James Horn of the University of Sussex, is reproduced in J.S. Moore (ed), *Avon Local History Handbook* (Chichester, 1979), p. 24.

22 The Public Record Office, however, intends to see through to conclusion the listing of P.C.C. Inventories, and some completed lists are already available in the *List and Index Society Series,* e.g. PROB. 3 (vols. 85–6), 5 (vol. 149). The Borthwick Institute, the Cornwall Record Office and a few other county record offices are listing their probate records as staffing permits.

23 C. Carlton, *The Court of Orphans* (Leicester, 1974); *cp.* M. Spufford, *loc. cit.*

24 Dr Sheila Marriner is engaged in listing the Bankruptcy records in the P.R.O. with support from the E.S.R.C.: see S. Marriner, 'English Bankruptcy Records and Statistics before 1850' (*Econ. Hist. Rev.* 2nd ser. vol. 33 (1980),

pp. 351–66). The only printed work that I know drawing on the non-probate inventories in the P.R.O. is A. Conyers, 'Wiltshire Extents for Debts, Edward I – Elizabeth I' *(Wiltshire Rec. Soc.,* vol. 28, 1973).

25   Early fire-insurance policy registers are also being listed with support from the E.S.R.C. by B.E. Supple and R.C. Floud: see also S.D. Chapman, 'The Devon Cloth Industry in the Eighteenth Century: Sun Fire Office Inventories of Merchants' and Manufacturers' Property, 1726–70' *(Devon and Cornwall Rec. Soc.* vol. 23, 1978)'. Surviving policy registers are listed in H.A.L. Cockerell, E. Green, *The British Insurance Business, 1547–1970: an Introduction and Guide to Historical Records in the United Kingdom* (1976), pp.76–118, 122–7.

26   J.S. Moore, *op. cit,* p.1 and references cited in nn. 2–3; see also R. Grassby, 'The Personal Wealth of the Business Community in 17th Century England' *(Econ. Hist. Rev.* vol. 23 (1970), pp. 220–34); J.A. Yelling, 'Probate Inventories and the Geography of Livestock Farming . . . (in) E. Worcestershire, 1540–1750', *(Trans. Instit. Brit. Geog.,* vol. 51 (1970). pp. 111–26); J.A. Yelling, 'The Combination and Rotation of Crops in East Worcestershire, 1540–1660' *(Agric. Hist. Rev.,* vol. 17 (1969), pp. 24–43); D. Hey, 'The Use of Probate Inventories for Industrial Archaeology' *(Ind. Arch.* vol. 10 (1973), pp. 200–13).

27   The periodicals *Post-Medieval Archaeology* and *Vernacular Architecture* as well as the publications of the Vernacular Architecture Group are an invaluable corrective to a too exclusively document-centred approach to history, though one often wonders whether some archaeologists and architectural historians have ever heard of, let alone looked at, documents.

28   J.S. Moore, *op. cit,* pp. 34–5; the only work I know that attempts to deal adequately with the clothing of craftsmen and labourers is P. Cunnington, C. Lucas, *Occupational Costume in England from the eleventh century to 1914* (1967).

29   J.S. Moore, *op. cit,* p. 37; C. Cipolla, *Literacy and the Development of the West* (1969), pp. 15, 20–2, 53–4, 61–4, 78–9, 98.

30   J.S. Moore, *op. cit,* pp. 37–8.

31   In addition to the publications of the *English Dialect Society,* see also J. Wright, *English Dialect Dictionary* (6 vols. 1898–1905). The result of the modern survey is contained in H. Orton, E. Dieth, *Survey of English Dialects* (Leeds, 13 vols. 1962–68); H. Orton, N. Wright, *A Word Geography of England* (1974); H. Orton, S. Sanderson, J. Widdowson, *The Linguistic Atlas of England* (1978).

PROBATE RECORDS AND THE KENDAL SHOEMAKERS IN THE SEVENTEENTH CENTURY

C.B. Phillips

The wide survival of probate records is both a measure of the institutional zeal of the church officials who administered probate, and of the shared fears, achievements and ambitions of the many folk, rich and not so rich, who drew up their wills, or helped to price a deceased person's goods. The motive for will making is not always clear. It was encouraged by those clerics who so often wrote the wills, and who helped to make known influential biblical examples to encourage people to look after their estates and provide for their families. It is touching but not surprising to find the people of Stockport making their wills in conscious imitation of 'Good King Hezekiah' who put his house in order when he was ill, and was spared by the Lord, and, at the other end of the spectrum of urban wealth, to find the rich Bristol merchant John Fowens citing in 1609 the exhortation of the prophet Isiah, who told Hezekiah to put his house in order. We can only wish that more had heeded their example, or followed those testators who eschewed biblical comparison but declared their intention to preserve amity in the family by making a will instead of dying intestate.[1]

The process of probate, and the form of the records, in the Deanery of Kendal, part of the Archdeaconry of Richmond, a quasi-independent part of the Diocese of Chester, followed that prevailing elsewhere in the northern Province. The deceased's executors or administrators approached the local official responsible for probate, and, normally, presented a will in order to take letters of administration. On the same day they entered a bond to

administer the deceased's estate and perform the will, and to exhibit
to the court an inventory of his goods, debts and credits (which they
had usually already had made), and to make an account of their
administration. For Kendal the most frequent documents to survive
are wills and inventories; in the period covered in this paper,
1580–1700, bonds are more numerous after the first quarter of the
seventeenth century, and probate accounts are few and far between,
perhaps because they were rarely made, as rough calculations on the
back of inventories suggest. Table I details the survival of cordwainers' records.[2]

The uses to which these documents have been put by historians
are as wide as their content. At one extreme we have the detailed
study of a mid-Essex manor by the late Francis Steer, at the other
extreme, the work published in 1979 by Dr Mark Overton involving
the computerized analysis of 14,000 East Anglian inventories in
pursuit of grain prices and yields.[3] My paper today will follow many
of the well trodden paths, but I want also to look at the problems of
inflation in the period as it affects values given in inventories in
order to find a way of comparing the inventories of different people
or groups of people. In quantifying the evidence in this way I realise
that I am replacing one imperfect picture of the raw evidence by
another imperfect picture, but one which offers a further dimension
of the past. Quantification in sixteenth- and seventeenth-century
history is not an exact science: there are problems in my case with
the size and randomness of the sample. I claim no exactitude in
trying to obviate the distortion which inflation in those years creates
for the historian with comparative interests, but I think the method
is helpful, and I would like your views on it in discussion after.

The last purpose of these introductory remarks is to explain why I
want to study the probate records of the Kendal shoemakers. This
arises from the present state of my research on the town of Kendal,
in which I need to examine a relatively lowly status group in that
town, both because of the intrinsic interest of such a group, and in
order to make comparisons and contrasts with other status groups in
the town, especially the corporation. But humble though the
shoemakers may have been in most towns – they were for example
debarred from the corporation at Norwich, together with other
artisan groups – they were part of one of the major industries of pre-
or proto-industrial England: the leather industry. They were also
freemen, and that means that there were many people in the town of

Kendal below them on the social and economic scale. I have included as cordwainers people not so called in their probate records, but who can be identified as such from the content of their inventory, and other records, including the list of freemen cordwainers.[4] I have in this context included some 'retired' cordwainers, at least one of whom called himself yeoman.

The Kendal cordwainers were amongst the original guilds or companies founded at the town's incorporation in 1575. The first list of freemen cordwainers, dated to *ca.* 1580, enumerates at maximum 38 men. Numbers fluctuated: probably 14 in 1641; lists of the 1660's suggest about 26; in 1649 there were 34 members but only 19 of these were still members in 1700. There are no reliable lists for the early seventeenth century, but I count 21 cordwainers alive in 1620, and 38 alive in 1630. Not counting those alive in 1700, between 1575 and 1700 there were 224 cordwainers. How many probate records for these men are now extant? There is available some form of probate document for 55 of these men, 24.6%; 48 inventories are extant, for 21.4% of the group. These figures compare tolerably well with a survival rate of 23.2% for inventories of 82 Kendal adults (that is, males and single and widowed women only) who died n the calendar year January 1622/3–December 1623.[6] A further but inexact comparison is with the figure of 37% survival for some sort of probate document for a random sample of the surnames in the index to the Kendal *Boke off Record* covering the years 1575–

TABLE I

Extant probate records for Kendal Cordwainers 1580–1700

will, inventory and bond(s)	23
inventory and bond(s)	12
will and inventory	6
inventory only	4
will only	3
will and bond(s)	2
inventory, bond(s) and account	2
inventory and account	1
account only	1
bond only	1
	——
	55

c. 1676.[7] Once made, there is no reason to think anything other than chance governed the survival of the cordwainers' probate records, and therefore, and this is important, the surviving documents can be considered as typical of the probate documents of the Kendal cordwainers as a whole. Unlike some higher status groups all but one of the cordwainers proved their wills in the deanery of Kendal, so that we do not have to face the problems caused by the loss of the inventories of the prerogative courts.[8]

Nothing in the probate records of the Kendal cordwainers suggests that they operated in any way differently to the general scheme of the leather industry established by Dr Clarkson for pre-industrial England.[9] The cordwainers bought leather from the tanners, for the inventories do not indicate that they tanned any hides themselves. The presence of 'dressed and undressed leather' in some inventories, and reference in others to 'hides at the curriers' indicates that the cordwainers then sent their leather to be softened and waterproofed by the curriers. Finally, the shoemakers shaped the leather into shoes or boots. Dr Clarkson, rightly, was careful to emphasize that this was only the normal division of occupations in the shoe trade. Possibly the norm was modified marginally at Kendal in three ways. Firstly there are some references to 'lymed heads' in inventories, that is, small pieces of leather being cleaned of hair at the first stage of tanning process. Secondly, there were very few *men* admitted freemen of Kendal as curriers before 1700. Most Kendal cordwainers probably curried their own leather, like James Troughton the elder (1595) whose inventory included train oil and tallow suitable for that purpose. Thirdly, and here the evidence is ambiguous, it may be that some cordwainers made leather by the unskilled 'dressing' process, a method quite separate from the making of leather by tanning. This light leather may have been used for the upper works of the more fancy boots and shoes, and even for the 'slippers' which Christopher Woodburne had in his cordwainer's shop at his death in 1665. The raw materials for this dressed leather may have been the calf 'skins' referred to in inventories, although these equally could have been tanned. Furthermore, the 'lymed heads' may have been being cleaned prior to dressing.

One of the largest stocks, in varied sizes, of completed shoes was that of Richard Wilson (1623), with 90 pairs of shoes in six sizes worth £4 4s 0d, and 36 'little' shoes worth 9s 0d. John Cowper (1637) had 14 pairs of boots worth £3 and a gross of 'new' pairs of shoes (did he have old shoes?)[10] worth £11 4s 0d. Not all the inventories enumerated the stock, but Edward Nicholson (1633) with 3½ dozen pair of shoes had one of the smallest. Roger Askew (1636) carried 34 [pairs of] mens clogs £1 6s 9d, 47 womens' clogs, £1 7s 5d, and 41 ladys' [? lads] clogs, 16s 5d. Apart from Christopher Woodburne's slippers already mentioned, the only other type of shoe stocked in Kendal was the pointed–toed pike. Such specialist items as slippers, pikes, even boots, suggests a bespoke trade, and perhaps we should not think of all the shoe stocks as 'ready to wear' items. The appearance of a few local gentry, and some Kendal aldermen, as debtors for a few shillings in inventories perhaps indicates bespoke transactions. Thus John Sadler (1629) was owed 2s 6d by Mr George Midleton (son of Thomas Midleton of Leighton esquire) and 5s 8d by Mr Henry Parke, one time alderman of Kendal. It was probably to cater for such a bespoke trade that John Cowper (1637) carried red and black leather, while William Hollhead (1599) and William Postlethwaite (1689) carried, respectively, red and black leather. The 'couching' which appears with the over (leather for upper works) in some inventories and which refers to fancy inlays and overlays in the leather of boots and shoes again evidences the practice of bespoke work, although elaborate designs on 'ready to wear' work was not impossible.

Such fancies were doubtless worked with the aid of the marking irons (only found in sixteenth-century inventories) and with awls or pricks, found in most inventories. These piercing tools facilitated the stitching, apparently done with hemp yarn and then proofed with wax or rosin. But what was steel-hemp, and what did Thomas Barrow (1688) use it for? The other tools were unremarkable: cutting boards and blocks (for both beating work on and storing awls etc), hammers, saws, planes (for shaving the leather in the currying stage) various knives, lasts, boot-trees, wax and liquor pans, sharpening stones and even a shoe horn all appear in the inventories. Most cordwainers had seats in their shops, and cushions for their backsides! Such tools and materials were inexpensive: James Troughton's were worth £2 12s 0d in 1596, but he had leather and shoes worth £28; Nicholas Docker (1668)'s tools included cushions for the seats but only came to 10s 0d compared to stock valued at £8 10s 0d.

Questions such as where the tanned leather came from; or, who bought the shoes, expose the limitations of the Kendal probate inventories. It is the debts listed in the inventories which are the most helpful here. Out of 49 inventories only four list a debt owed specifically to a tanner, perhaps evidence that the debt was incurred for leather. But only one of the four states explicitly that the debt was incurred for leather. In other instances, creditors listed have the same name as a Kendal tanner, but that does not take us very far. In 1633 Edward Nicholson owed John Atkinson for bend leather, but there was no John Atkinson amongst the Kendal tanners. We can measure the extent of our ignorance by looking at another source. The rolls of the Kendal corporation Court of Record give details of some transactions between tanners and Kendal cordwainers in the Kendal market; most, but not all, of the tanners were also Kendal men. In the late sixteenth and early seventeenth centuries it is clear that cordwainers commonly bought tanned hides by the dicker or by the single hide, and on credit (for up to a year) with more than one credit transaction outstanding, or for cash. Indeed, one cordwainer, for whom no probate records survive, one Thomas Postlethwaite, had a running account with a Kendal sadler/tanner, William Wallace. The court rolls, however, are as unhelpful as the inventories when we look at the sale of shoes. There are no court roll cases about shoe sales, but one explicit inventory, that of Nicholas Docker (1668), shows that Thomas Beck of Staveley owed him 5s 6d for a pair of shoes; Mathew Braithwaite owed 3s 0d for one pair, Robert Lickbarrow 4s 0d for shoes, and Thomas Borrick £4 8s 0d for shoes. But there is no indication as to where these three men lived, perhaps in Kendal as we are told that Beck lived outside Kendal in Staveley? Did Thomas Borrick buy £4 8s 0d worth of shoes at once, or was that sum a cumulative debt? Credit transactions in shoe sales were probably as routine as they were in leather purchases, and sales credit was given to ordinary men. For example in 1590 Edward Braithwaite, a blacksmith, owed Thomas Eskrigg 5s 0d for a pair of boots. We are not told where Braithwaite lived, although others of Eskrigg's debtors lived in north Westmorland, a clue to the geography of that Kendal cordwainer's trade.

Thomas Eskrigg only took one apprentice, who was no longer with him in 1590. His probate records make no reference to journeymen cordwainers, and it is likely that Eskrigg had made those boots of Edward Braithwaite's himself. But shoemaking was a labour intensive industry, with little scope for labour saving except skill and practice; making more shoes meant employing more men or taking on more apprentices. Probate records are not the best source for apprentices – there are more systematic records amongst the archives of the shoemaker's guild. But probate records give incidental clues to the use of journeymen, something on which the guild records are silent. William Hollhead's will of 1599 tells us that he had two 'servants'. When he died in 1665 Christopher Woodburne owed one journeyman 2s 0d and other, unspecified, servants, £1 13s 4d. From a subsequent lawsuit we learn that he employed at least one more journeyman, his own son William who was claiming arrears of wages from his father's estate.[12] Edmund Hartley had three 'servants' at his death in 1677, and in 1688 Thomas Barrow's will mentioned three. Two of Hartley's men had been freemen cordwainers for eight years, and were described as 'cordwainers' by Hartley in his will, while the third was out of his apprenticeship; two of Barrow's men were sworn freemen in the year of his death, the third had no apparent connection with the company. The probate records here throw light on the number of journeymen employed, but also raise the interesting question about the employment for wages of freemen cordwainers.

If the probate records suggest nothing peculiar about the craft habits of Kendal cordwainers, they do suggest that by their deaths five cordwainers were no longer following that trade. One was aged 75, and had little of anything. Two others, one aged, the other 56, had considerable interests in farm land; another, although aged 76, had cloth worth £13 in stock. Whether the circumstances of these men are explained in each case by their advanced age, or whether these interests in land and textiles outside the shoe trade represent the culmination of trends which developed earlier in their lives is difficult to say. That the latter may have been the case is indicated by the inventories of Robert Wharton (1685), William French (1677) and Anthony Hudson (1690), who all had substantial assets in other trades besides shoemaking. Wharton was a linen merchant of some substance with linen cloth and raw materials worth £32 13s 8d compared with only £6 14s 10d in shoemaking, a trade which he nevertheless actively pursued. French had £12 worth of wool, nearly double the value of his shoemaker's goods; Hudson had £8 tied up in drink in his tavern, nearly half the value of his shoemaker's goods. Twelve more cordwainers had a subsidiary textile interest, although these rarely amounted to more than the possession of a loom; three of the twelve possessed hemp, but was it for their thread or for linen cloth? So, 15 people had another commercial interest in addition to shoemaking, furthermore the inventories of 13 of these men include some agricultural items; and altogether 35 of the 49 cordwainers inventories include some agricultural element. For 28 men this interest amounted only to the possession of a cow and some hay, perhaps a few pigs, some poultry and a horse (probably for transport rather than agriculture). Whatever the proportion of the value of their inventory which such items represented, such men clearly did not have a major interest in agriculture. Of the seven cordwainers who did have a larger interest in agriculture one man had hay, two cows, four horses, some swine and a barn. But the six others were all practising arable agriculture as well as having a few stock – one of these men, Anthony Hudson (1690) had £8 worth of drink, as we have seen. Judged by the proportion of his inventory wealth shoemaking was more important to Hudson than his tavern, but less than his agriculture; his son Anthony who died in 1699, was the only other cordwainer in this group for whom agriculture was more important than shoes.

There remain eleven cordwainers with no additional trade to shoes, and no interest in agriculture. We know little about three of these men, and they must be left on one side. Four of them had no real estate in possession, and were living in lodgings, which explains their lack of agricultural interests. But three of these men had another source of income from lending money by bond or on mortgage. A fourth had some malt in his house and may have brewed ale to sell. A fifth man derived a small income from rental and we shall have to return to real estate later. Before that we need to survey the manual economic interests of the cordwainers, with the rest of their families in mind as well as the cordwainers themselves.

Firstly let us forget about the 'retired' cordwainers. Of the rest, the practising cordwainers, nine had major interests besides shoemaking: one had two alternatives; six were significantly involved in agriculture and two in textiles. We can understand these men taking time off from shoemaking to devote to their other trades, and bringing in journeymen or apprentices to make shoes. In fact labour was sometimes hired to work the alternative interest: thus shoemaker William Hollhead (1599) owed 6s 0d to Nicholas Hodshon for ploughing an acre of ground. The other interests, especially agriculture, could have been looked after by the cordwainer's wife and children, indeed it is tempting to see them looking after the spinning of wool, and even hemp. But did the wives or children work the looms which eight cordwainers owned? Women and children no doubt looked after the odd cow and the pigs which 27 cordwainers had, but only one cordwainer's inventory mentioned cheese, so dairying was not important. Two owned a cow and calf – which might indicate stock rearing. But it is difficult to see either making much profit, or consuming much of the family's time. Journeymen were hired to supplement the master's labour in shoe making, as we have seen, so family labour was not utilized in that way. What then did the families of these men do? The probate records raise the question for wives and for children, up to the age until they were apprenticed or put to service, indeed they make the question stand out by failing to provide an answer.

In contrast to what has gone before, I want now to try to derive from the inventories an idea of the cordwainer's overall wealth. There are a numer of difficulties inherent in such an approach, of which the most basic are that the cordwainers, like any group of men, did not die at the same point in their lives, some were old, some young, most middle aged; and that they died in different years. As a result, the nature, as well as the order of their wealth differs the one from the other. Statistically, these points would matter less if there was a larger body of evidence. Nevertheless, the assumption behind what follows is that the surviving records are typical of the cordwainers as a whole.

To construct Table II, I have calculated the proportion of a cordwainer's goods which comprised stock-in-trade, agricultural items, household goods, and ready cash and plate, and expressed each category as a percentage of the value of his total goods (excluding debts). Stock-in-trade includes raw materials and finished shoes in stock, and tools of the trade; agriculture includes animals and crops and husbandry gear, but not prepared foodstuffs stored in the house – which may have been purchased rather than farmed; household goods comprises everything else except plate and ready money. Stock-in-trade includes the linen cloth, wool, and drink held by those with the major alternative trade interests that I have mentioned, and household goods includes the interests in textiles also discussed above. The table itself lists the median values of these percentages, divided into two chronological periods, from 1580 to 1649 – a period of high inflation – and from 1660 to 1700, a period of fluctuating rather than inflationary price change. Table II also gives for the same chronological periods the median in £ of the total value of goods, but at values deflated to a base at the decade 1570–1579.[13] Price changes in the period 1580–1700 varied enormously, and differed as between commodities. The bulk of the goods in these inventories are industrial products – household goods and stock in trade. Price changes in leather brought about a slower rise of prices than in textiles in the late sixteenth century, for example. Generally, the rise of industrial prices was much lower than the rise in food prices, probably because the price rise was caused by population pressure which increased demand for food while reducing wage costs. There is no evidence of technical innovation in our industry which might have led to a reduction in prices. It follows therefore that the value of a cordwainer's goods in, say, 1590, must be compared with those of one who died in 1640 in real terms rather than as inventory values. To achieve such a real comparison it is necessary to deflate the inventory values to a common base. This is a perilous operation, for we have no evidence of local price levels for Kendal, the only price series we have reflects conditions in southern England, which may or may not differ from prices in Kendal. Neither is there available a price index sensitive to differences between industrial and agricultural prices for the whole of the seventeenth century, although there is one up to 1649. The best index available for the whole century is for the price of the Phelps Brown/Hopkins basket of consumables, which includes, primarily, agricultural items, with some industrial products. While this index most probably misrepresents the detailed changes in prices in Kendal, provided that we apply it only to Kendal men we are, at worst, using an arbitrary but common deflationary factor on the inventories which will be at its weakest in portraying chronological trends.[14]

Now let us look at Table II. The most suspect figures, the medians of total value of goods, suggest that the cordwainers were better off in the latter rather than the earlier period, figures of £32.63 and £18.5 respectively. The medians of the percentage distribution of wealth, which are not affected by the deflation process, being calculated from current prices, tend to confirm this view. In the late seventeenth century the cordwainers could afford to put more of their wealth into the content of their houses, and needed to carry less in stock; with prices steady, cash in hand was safer than it had

TABLE II

Kendal Cordwainers 1580–1700: Wealth in Inventories

Proportion of value of goods, in specified categories, expressed as medians

	% Money	% Hsehld.	% Agric.	% Trade
1580–1650	5.9	33.1	8.4	47.3
1660–1700	13.1	43.1	12.4	28.85

Medians of total value of goods, deflated to 1570–79

	£
1580–1650	18.5
1660–1700	32.63

been in the earlier period, and consequently the cordwainers held more. In general, the view that the cordwainers were enjoying a better standard of living in the later seventeenth century is what we would expect, for the cost of food, of which most cordwainers produced little, was low.

It is appropriate now to return to the moneylending habits and real estate interests of the cordwainers, alluded to before, because it may be objected that the picture suggested by Table II ignores these two forms of wealth. A few title deeds survive for properties once owned by cordwainers, but most information about their real estate comes from probate records. What we do learn from title deeds, law suits and other sources does not conflict with the picture which emerges from a study of the probate records. A cordwainer needed a shop, chiefly to work in, perhaps to sell from, and also possibly a market stall. A Kendal cordwainer's shop was usually integral with his house, and if he carried much leather a store room or 'leather-house' would also be required; any room would do. The cow or horse would need a stable, but otherwise the cordwainer's economy needed no special property. Even those who practised a little agriculture may have used a 'barn' or 'croft' which, like their stable, was parcel of their tenement. Indeed one title deed of a cordwainer refers to corn growing on his tenement in Kendal.[15] However, some barns were 'on the Fell'. Only four cordwainers held agricultural land which was clearly not part of their tenement. Six held more than one tenement in Kendal, and four held a tenement outside Kendal in addition to one in the town. One of the 'retired' cordwainers had, 20 years before his death, been one of three partners who had leased the corporation's weight loft and scales.[16] Thus most cordwainers held the same amount of real estate, so that while this wealth is not encompassed by Table II, its absence is not a major distortion.

Money owed to the deceased is not included in Table II either. Inventories were supposed to include the debts and credits of the deceased, and this was made explicit in the wording of the bond prescribed in the text of the 1671 act for the administration of intestate estates. But in the sixteenth and early seventeenth centuries it was not uncommon for debts and credits to be listed in wills. Even after that, the recording of debts and credits in inventories was inconsistent. Altogether, 15 inventories make no mention of debts owed to the deceased, seven do not mention debts owed by the deceased, and four omit any mention of either category. Here the historian is reminded most forcibly that probate inventories were not created to facilitate the work of future historians; they were created to delimit the liabilities of the deceased's executors. This is made clear if we look at the probate accounts which should have been submitted by the deceased's executors to the church court. In all, I have accounts for twenty-two Kendal residents in this period, including four cordwainers. These accounts show that the executors were charged with the sum of the deceased's inventory, which they could discharge by claiming their expenses and by listing debts paid on behalf of the deceased. In the northern Province in this period the distribution of the residue, if any, was controlled by custom, which seems generally, but not invariably, to have been followed. Once an executor had paid out money up to the level of the charge, then he could ask for his discharge by the church court, even though he would remain liable in common law for any outstanding debts, and in equity, for unpaid shares of the deceased's estate, especially in cases of intestacy; in the latter instance the discharge by the church courts did not always prevent the bringing of lawsuits in Chancery. In these circumstances there was a real incentive for the executor to conceal debts owing to the deceased. That there were such allegedly unscrupulous executors is made clear by the level of litigation in Chancery in the seventeenth century, and by the 1671 act.[17]

The question before us is whether or not, in the absence of debts and credits in an inventory, it is safe to assume that there were no such items. Probate accounts show the existence of such items where the inventory does not mention them, and, even where debts were listed in the inventory, add further details. Thus for the cordwainer Robert Wharton (1665), whose inventory listed no debts, we find that he owed £88 5s 0d; no debts owed to Wharton are given in the account. These debts exceeded Wharton's inventoried assets (£68 16s 10d) by £19 11s 5d which, nevertheless, his executor paid. The answer to our question is that in the absence of debts or credits we cannot assume that there were none. It follows that the recording of debts and credits by inventories was inconsistent, and this means trouble for the historian seeking to use inventories in a quantitative manner. In our case it throws doubt on the overall picture presented in Table II, for 18 cordwainers were owed large sums of money which are not represented in Table II.

Unfortunately, the inventories of nine of these 18 men give only totals, and are thus uninformative. In six cases however the greater part of the debts owing to the cordwainer, varying from the entire £125 owed to William Woodburne (1696) to £120 out of £129 2s 2d of good debts owed to William Postlethwaite (1689) was owed by bond or specialty. That is, the debts were not from the routine debt book entries for the sale of shoes. In the other three cases no less than half was on bond; for example John Hartley (1677) was owed £84 8s 9d: £56 in bonds, £6 15s 0d by his debt book, and the rest in small sums by named persons. These large sums lent on bond suggest not massive purchases of shoes on credit secured by bond, but money lending. Indeed the prisers of John Hartley's inventory specifically stated that more was due to the executor in interest on the bonds.

The issue now is whether we must include debts and credits in our overall view of the cordwainer's wealth in Table II. Inclusion would be most imperative were we sure that all these sums arose from the trade of the deceased. In the example of the shoemakers this is not the case, although it may be so for other trades, especially wholesalers. The strongest argument for excluding debts and credits from Table II is the inconsistent nature of the record. Furthermore, some of the most substantial bondholders had no real estate – their bonds were the equivalent of the average cordwainer's single tenement. Were we to decide to include them (and I have decided not to!), there remains the question of how to represent the sums involved? If we adopted the net calculation beloved of executors and the church courts in their probate accounts, that is goods plus credits, less debts, we should bankrupt 13 cordwainers, perhaps unrealistically, for that course postulates a liquidation of their assets which presumably never took place. It is the case that many historians have represented total values of probate inventories in this manner. But debts owed by the deceased are more than a list of his liabilities, they are a measure of his credit in the community, the extent to which he was allowed to incur debts. It follows that a gross expression of the inventory figures, goods plus credits, *plus* debts, might offer us a better insight.

The wills of the cordwainers, especially when coupled with town and guild records, can tell us a lot about these men and their families. The administration bond for Thomas Barrow (1688), and his will, show that he came from Cartmel in Lancashire. Between 1645 and 1680 some 101 apprentices were accepted by the cordwainers, according to both town and guild records.[18] Thirty nine per cent of these were children of Kendal men, 42% came from outside the town, and the origins of 30% are not stated. Most of those who came from outside the town were from Westmorland (24%), with 13% from Furness and a few from West Yorkshire and Cumberland. A sizeable number of the apprentices from Kendal homes were the sons of shoemakers. We can see this family tradition also by the presence of dynasties of cordwainers in the town across much of our period. The great surnames of shoemaking in Kendal from the late sixteenth century were Backhouse, Cowper, Hartley, Troughton and Woodburne. But these surnames are deceptive, for more than one family had the same surname. Thus there is no proven relationship between James Troughton the elder, and James Troughton the younger, two prominent cordwainers who died at the end of the sixteenth century, nor between them and James Troughton sworn free in 1626, Edward Troughton sworn 1618, and John Troughton sworn in 1594. Nevertheless John Troughton represents a century of Troughton involvement in Kendal shoemaking. He must have been apprenticed about 1587; his son Miles, also a cordwainer although he called himself yeoman in his will, died in 1690. Thomas Hartley was apprenticed in 1605 to Edmund Hartley: I am uncertain whether the two were related. Thomas died in 1644 but was followed in the trade by three of his four sons (if the fourth one lived to become a freeman he was probably a butcher). Two of Thomas's grandchildren were cordwainers in 1700. But there is another demographic experience apparent. Leonard Cowper became a cordwainer freeman in 1606. The youngest of his three sons died unmarried. The second son, a cordwainer, died without children in 1637, and the eldest son, also a cordwainer, died leaving two daughters in 1655.[19] So the Cowper involvement in the trade, by the accidents of birth and mortality, lasted only a few years longer than the lifespan of Leonard, who died in 1643. Nine wills show no male heir, other evidence also points to that circumstance, and so it is clear that the Cowper experience was not unique.

Most of the cordwainers married soon after becoming freemen, although the interval could be as long as five years. It follows that their age at marriage was as high as the national average, and higher if the cordwainers had served time as journeymen. One surprising point is that few cordwainers married the daughters of cordwainers. Probate records turn up only two marriage connections with cordwainers, both in the Cowper family: Leonard Cowper's sister married a cordwainer, and Leonard's daughter Anne married the cordwainer John Rowlandson. The bulk of the probate records, supported by the parish register, show that these were unusual links.[20]

Bequest by will was one of the usual ways of passing on real estate, and the cordwainers' wills are a reminder to us that the lower orders of society also saw an economic dimension to marriage. The marriage settlements of the landed gentry are paralleled by similar settlements amongst the Kendal cordwainers. Thus when he died in 1637 the childless John Cowper bequeathed to his father his interest in the tenement which his father had settled on him at his marriage, provided that there was no posthumous child. John provided for his widow out of his personal estate, and apparently she had no interest in the tenement. When James Chamber married his second wife she brought with her a tenement. James bequeathed (1615) that to her and her daughter. Chamber's other tenement, outside Kendal, was to be sold to pay debts, but James Chamber's mother was to have that part of the sale price which had been 'agreed before Mr Green and Mr Martin', who had arbitrated to preserve the old widow's rights. Real estate passed to women when widowed by custom in Kendal, although a husband had discretion in making detailed arrangements.[21] As most cordwainers only had one tenement, however, they had little room for manoeuvre. Six out of the 34 cordwainers' wills make no mention of real estate, but in the others any widow received a tenement for her widowhood. In most instances where there was a male heir the property passed to the eldest son (often the only surviving son although in one case two brothers were given one burgage each, and, in another, two shared one burgage). In two instances daughters were given equal shares with the sons. Only when there was no male heir were daughters likely to inherit real property, with the testators' brothers or their children the next favoured relations.

Another insight into the lives of the Kendal shoemakers which probate records offer is into literacy, or at least their ability to sign their name. In fact the cordwainers' guild records are the best guide to the literacy of these men. Signatures assenting to orders in the guild books (Table III) suggest that the cordwainers' literacy improved as the seventeenth century progressed, although we need further evidence before this trend can be regarded as established. The probate records show that this was not the case for their wives. Twenty-four authentifications of probate bonds show only two widows, and one daughter, who could sign their name; the other 21 made a mark. If the cordwainers were well schooled, their wives were not. Both those cordwainers who came from Kendal, and those who migrated to the town had good educational opportunities, for Westmorland was especially well endowed with schools at this time. Nevertheless, by the evidence of their inventories few cordwainers owned books besides the bible and other church books such as a psalter. James Atkinson, in 1690, had books in the kitchen loft worth £1; probably he could read for he signed his will. At the start of the period in 1581 Anthony Backhouse had a bible, psalter and other books worth 14s 0d. More interesting are the books of 'false doctrine' which James Troughton bequeathed to Mr Ingall, the Grammar School master, to take away in 1599.

Other evidence of the possession of luxuries by the cordwainers, as an indication of their standard of living, is available in their wills and inventories. One of the best housed must have been William French who died in 1677. His inventory conveys an impression of comfort and warmth, with fires in at least two rooms; he also owned a bible, and another luxury item, a looking glass. Where details of bedding are given in the inventory, it is clear that chaff beds predominated, but at both the beginning and end of our period some cordwainers had feather beds. Few cordwainers had much in the way of plate: Christopher Woodburne (1665) and William Postlethwaite (1689) with £3 each had the most. Two cordwainers lived in 'new' houses, but most probably lived in older houses which, their inventories indicate, comprised a large hall floored and partitioned to provide more closed rooms, warmth and privacy. Such generalizations are probably best left to architectural historians, but it is certainly clear that most cordwainers had houses with large numbers of rooms, excluding workshops, leather stores and stables. Only four inventories before 1650 give the names of rooms. After 1660 the median of the number of rooms in sixteen inventories lies between eight and nine, between extremes of 14 and 4. Many of these rooms are described as lofts, sometimes appropriated for the servants or the maids, but others are obviously family rooms, with windows.

TABLE III

Signatures of Cordwainers in Guild Books*

	Mark	Sign	Query
1641	8	6	–
1663a	7	19	2
1663b	8	21	–
1701	1	11	–

*The books are cited in note 4

TABLE IV

Kendal Corporation 1575–1635: Occupational Structure

No. of freemen c.1580	Occupation	No. of corp. members 1575–1635
44	Distributive trades	37
201	Textiles (all shearmen)	12
76	Leather trades	7
40	Food	4
28	Metal trades	3
1	Professions (all attorneys)	2
		65

So much for the probate records of the Kendal cordwainers. What comparisons can we make between the Kendal shoemakers and other residents of the town and between shoemakers in Kendal and elsewhere? Clearly a full answer to this question would necessitate the use of material other than probate records, but the probate records can give us some clues. In Kendal the cordwainers as a group were much less wealthy than those citizens who comprised the corporation of the town, something that we might expect but which needs to be demonstrated. Individual cordwainers however did become members of one or both tiers of the corporation of Kendal, so the difference between shoemakers and members of the corporation was not an absolute one. In fact only two cordwainers reached the higher level of the corporation before 1650, but then only four tanners and one sadler were in the corporation (see Table IV). In general, only about half a dozen manual tradesmen reached the top of the corporation, except for the shearmen, the principal textile trade in Kendal, more of whose members reached that peak. The bulk of the corporation men were mercers or merchants, engaged in wholesale and retail distriubution. In terms of wealth, reflected in the net values of inventories deflated to a common base (the decade 1570–79), the cordwainers were clearly the poorest group, as Table V shows, when compared to the corporation, all the mercers, and all the shearmen (including those mercers and shearmen who were members of the corporation). Probate inventories here give us a useful tool of comparison with which to examine different groups in Kendal. They are better in this respect than tax returns, which in Kendal as in any other town are suspect indicators of corporation wealth. The corporation men either avoided the tax, or, more frequently, paid it at a higher rate than the generality.[23] In any case the use of tax returns as indicators of wealth is a hazardous business. The figures in Table V are calculated on a different basis to those in Table II. The index used is more sensitive to industrial prices, and the Table V figures are based on net values of probate inventories, because this value is what other historians have most frequently used.[24] In fact the net figures, with their apparent bankruptcies, show that the corporation men operated on the largest scale in trade, for they were not only the most wealthy, but also the most bankrupt!

If the Kendal cordwainers were amongst the least wealthy, I say amongst for there were shearmen of the same order of wealth, then how did they compare with shoemakers of other towns? A few probate inventories of Banbury cordwainers between 1570 and 1590 and between 1621 and 1650 suggest a similar order of wealth, which is surprising for Banbury at this time had not begun to suffer from the growth of specialist shoemaking in nearby Northampton.[25] The dangers of such comparisons are perhaps well illustrated here, for it may be that the more wealthy Banbury cordwainers proved their wills in the Prerogative Court of Canterbury.[26] The inventories of sixteen Chester shoemakers studied by Donald Woodward suggest that they were more wealthy than the Kendal men, but then Chester was a specialist leather town so that we may expect a difference.[27] Another specialist centre, Leicester, however looks to have produced cordwainers who were poorer as a whole than their Kendal counterparts, despite the fact that the Leicester Cordwainers' company, at least until the mid-seventeenth century, was able to dominate the leather trade in that town.[28]

TABLE V

Kendal Corporation 1575–1635: Financial Status of Alderman and 12 Burgesses

Net Inventory Totals to a Base of 1570–79 = 223

Group	Net inventory figure			Positive Invs.		All Invs.	
	Max	Min	Max Neg	Ave	Median	Ave	Median
	£	£	£	£	£	£	£
All Corporation (21)	724	16.8	–68.4 (3)	307.5	260	256.3	185
All Mercers (13) [7 Cp]	606.5	1.4	–64.9 (1)	192	100	172.2	50
All Shearmen (58) [4 Cp]	466.3	.3	– 9.4 (7)	59.3	16.8	51.6	14
All Cordwainers (18)	211	.5	– 9.8 (5)	44	11.3	30.3	9.15

based on deaths to 1650

I have tried in this paper to show what information probate records will yield about one particular trade and its practitioners and their families; the method can be applied to any group. By comparison with other sources I have also tried to point to some of the frustrations which arise from deficiencies in inventories. Nevertheless, we can learn how the shoemakers organized their trade, where raw materials came from, how the work was organised, and who purchased shoes. For most men shoemaking was a full time trade; few had substantial interests in other economic activities on a day to day basis. In general the cordwainers followed a specialized existence in late sixteenth- and seventeenth-century Kendal. There is no evidence as to how most of their families contributed to their wealth. Socially the cordwainers were not an isolated group for they comprised men who came from outside the town, as well as Kendal children, and there was relatively little inter-marriage amongst the shoemaking families. Generally the shoemakers owned their own house, and in the latter part of the period these were quite private in their internal arrangement. The problems of using inventories to suggest the level of wealth of the cordwainers in a systematic manner are probably greater than problems encountered in arriving at the conclusions so far offered. Nevertheless the use of deflated inventory values, in effect as a proxy for a precise statement of the shoemakers' wealth, has some advantages. It helps to confirm evidence suggesting an improvement in their position in the later seventeenth century, and it establishes a comparative picture of the cordwainers in Kendal society. Their status was relatively humble, but there were others like them, while a few of the cordwainers joined the ranks of the town's élite.

Notes

1   'Not Mynded . . . to dye intestate but willinge rather after the Example of good kinge Ezechias to sett my house and goods in Order. To the End that peace and Quietness may bee had and Imbraced amongst my wiefe Children and frends after my Decease'. Will of Richard Smith, husbandman, of Stockport, proved 10 March 1699/70 (Cheshire County Record Office, Chester); *Merchants and Merchandise in Seventeenth Century Bristol*, ed. P. Magrath (Bristol Record Soc., XIX, 1955), p.43. The Biblical reference is to II Kings 20, v.1. I owe the Stockport reference to the students of my extra-mural class there.
2   The probate records for the western deaneries of the Archdeaconry are housed in the Lancashire County Record Office, Preston. Sufficient reference to documents cited in the text is given by the date and Deanery name, i.e. Kendal. I am grateful to successive county archivists at Preston, and to their staff, for help in working on these documents.
3   *Farm and Cottage Inventories of Mid-Essex, 1635–1749*, ed. F.W. Steer (Chelmsford, 1950); M. Overton, 'Estimating Crop Yields from Probate Inventories: An example from East Anglia 1585–1735', *Journal of Economic History*, XXXIX, 1979.

4   There are no freemen rolls for Kendal. *A Boke off Record,* ed. R.S. Ferguson (C[umberland and] W[estmorland] A[ntiquarian and] A[rchaeological] S[ociety], Extra Series, VII, 1892) has what appears to be an incomplete list of freemen of the town who were cordwainers. There are two books of the Cordwainers guild in C[umbria County] R[ecord] O[ffice], Kendal, one in Kendal corporation archives, and one in a Kendal solicitor's archive (WD/Ag), which list members of the guild. I owe much to the archivist-in-charge at Kendal, Miss S. J. Macpherson, and to her staff. I am glad to acknowledge support from the Social Science Research Council in my work on Kendal.

5   Ferguson, *Boke off Record,* pp. 64–66, comparison with the MS in the corporation archives indicates the initial members; Cordwainer's guild records.

6   I have counted as children in the parish register those described as 'son of . . .', 'daughter of . . .', and as adults those not so described; 'wife of . . .' is similarly construed. Kendal parish register to 1631 is in print in five volumes of the Parish Register Section of the CWAAS.

7   I omitted, before taking the sample, non Kendal names, e.g. kings and judges.

8   Contrary to another paper at this seminar, there are no probate inventories surviving for the Exchequer Court of York for before 1688 (information from the Borthwick Institute of Historical Research, York). See note 19 below.

9   L.A. Clarkson, 'The Organisation of the English Leather Industry in the late sixteenth and seventeenth centuries', *Econ[omic] Hist[ory] Rev[iew]*, 2nd series, XIII, 1960.

10 Shoes in for repair, not the property of the cordwainer, should not be listed, so that cobbling is not covered by the probate records. But Roger Askew (1686) had some 'old' clogs in his inventory. Corporation records speak of Cordwainers *and* cobblers. (The seminar discussion on this point was most helpful.)

11 All but two inventories speak of 'pairs' of shoes, the two exceptions are of the sixteenth century: Ant. Backhouse (1581) and Wm. Hollhead (1599), Roger Askew's (1686) lists odd numbers of clogs which are not said to be pairs, his 'old' clogs are in pairs.

12 P[ublic] R[ecord] O[ffice], London, Chancery Proceedings, Bills and Answers, C.5/574/21.

13 I have used the annual index values, averaged for decades, given in E.H. Phelps Brown and S. V. Hopkins, 'Seven Centuries of the Prices of Consumables', *Economica*, n.s., XXIII, 1956, pp. 194–195, col.(1). The calculation is:

$$ £ \times \frac{317}{\text{decennial av. for date of death}} $$

I am grateful to my colleague Dr Theo Balderston for much patient discussion of this method. The decision to use it, and the calculations made, and thus any errors, are my responsibility.

14 For a recent discussion of the need to take inflation into account in financial matters see W.G. Bittle and R.T. Lane, 'Inflation and Philanthropy in England: A Re-assessment of W.K. Jordan's Data', *Econ. Hist. Rev.*, 2nd.

ser., XXIX (1976), and the discussion of that paper, which deals with a different circumstance from that before us, in *Econ. Hist. Rev.,* 2nd ser., XXXI (1978).

15 Kendal Corporation Archives, HMC box, deed poll: Robert Harrison to William Holmer, cordwainer (i.e. Wm. Helmore in Furguson *Boke off Record,* p.65), 4 April 1633.

16 Kendal Corporation Deeds, Bdle 7, indenture of lease, 11 Dec. 1673.

17 Such litigation is especially obvious in P.R.O., Chancery Proceedings, Bills and Answers, C.6. For the preliminaries to the 1671 Act, 22 & 23 Chas II. c.10 'An Act for the better setling of Intestates Estates', Historical Manuscripts Commission, *Eighth Report, Appendix,* Pt. I, pp 118(b), 122(a). For the custom of the north see, G.G. Alexander, 'The Custom of the Province of York', *Miscellanea* (Thoresby Society, XXVIII, 1928).

18 Kendal Corporation archives, Kendal apprentices book, 1645–1784; C.R.O. Kendal, WD/Ag Cordwainer's book. Outside these dates the records are less helpful.

19 Walter Copwer's will was proved, in the 1650's, at Canterbury, P.R.O., Prerogative Court of Canterbury, PROB. 11/246, f.201.

20 Wills of Walter Cowper (note 19), Leonard (1643) and John (1637): cordwainers' dates of freedom are given in Ferguson, *Boke off Record,* pp.64–66.

21 This statement is based on a reading of many Kendal wills besides those of cordwainers. Husbands could leave real property to their widow for life, or to the widow for life and then to her heirs or assigns. Sometimes more than one of these options was followed.

22 The absence of freemen rolls makes it difficult to put the coporation trade structure in perspective. Table IV includes therefore the numbers of founder members in each guild as listed in Ferguson, *Boke off Record,* pp.49–81 and compared with the MS. The trade structure used here follows that used by L.A. Clarkson, *The Pre-Industrial Economy in England, 1500–1750* (London, 1971), pp. 88–89.

23 Eg. Ferguson, *Boke off Record,* p.225, Cf. T. Pape, *Newcastle-under-Lyme in Tudor and Stuart Times* (Manchester, 1938), pp.278–279,281.

24 This table is calculated from the sum of the decennial indices for agricultural and industrial items, divided by two, given by P.J. Bowden, 'Statistical Appendix', in *The Agrarian History of England and Wales, vol. IV, 1500–1640,* ed. Joan Thirsk (Cambridge, 1967), p.862. The calculation is:

$$£ \times \frac{268}{\text{Dec. av. of Agric. \& Ind.}}$$

The agricultural/industrial element is used as a reflection of food costs and of the largely 'industrial' content of the inventories.

25 *Household and Farm Inventories in Oxfordshire, 1550–1590,* ed. M.A. Havinden (London, 1965); *Banbury Wills and Inventories, vol. II, 1621–1650,* ed. E.R.C. Brinkworth and J.S.W. Gibson (Banbury Historical Society, XIV, 1976); *V.C.H. Oxfordshire,* X, ed. A. Crossley (London, 1972), pp.63–64.

26 Havinden, *op.cit.,* p.5; Brinkworth & Gibson, *op.cit.,* appendix. In selecting

inventories care was taken to exclude those of Banbury parish not within the borough of Banbury, see *V.C.H. Oxfordshire,* X, p.5.

27 D.M. Woodward, 'The Chester Leather Industry, 1558–1625', *Transactions of the Historic Society of Lancashire and Cheshire,* CXIX, 1968, p.110.

28 E.W.J. Kerridge, 'The City of Leicester: Social and Economic History 1509–1680', *V.C.H. Leicestershire,* IV, ed. R.A. McKinley (London, 1958), pp.83–84 (citing inventories in Leicestershire Record Office).

INHERITANCE, WOMEN, RELIGION AND EDUCATION IN EARLY MODERN SOCIETY AS REVEALED BY WILLS

Nesta Evans

In the use of probate records by historians the emphasis has been placed on inventories rather than on wills. Perhaps the reason is that the former are more easily analyzed and provide detailed information about various aspects of the economic circumstances of our forbears. Fortunate are the historians whose chosen area of research is richly provided with sixteenth- and seventeenth-century probate inventories, but for those who work in less well endowed counties wills are a valuable adjunct to inventories. Not only do they cover the same ground, although less completely, but wills also provide information about a much wider range of subjects and, being more common, a larger number of people.

It is not uncommon for wills to contain considerable detail about furnishings, livestock and crops, the same field covered by inventories. Of course the items and animals bequeathed in a will can only be taken as the minimum owned by the testator, but some wills appear to be almost as full as inventories and the location of pieces of furniture is often recorded, thus giving some idea of the size of the deceased's house. Descriptions can be more detailed than in inventories: the colours and names of cows and horses, the wood of which furniture is made, the size and relative worth of utensils are all more likely to be found in wills than in inventories. Although both growing and harvested crops appear in wills, quantities are seldom given and it is rarely possible, at least in East Anglia, to deduce the total acreage owned by the testator. Students of costume find wills far more useful than inventories. In the latter clothes are usually listed as her or his apparel, but some wills, particularly those of women, go into considerable detail about articles of dress left as bequests.

Inventories deal with the material possessions of the dead, but wills allow us to look into their minds and to observe their thoughts, beliefs and sentiments. In addition much can be learnt about local charities, the repair and building of churches, the existence of long-vanished ecclesiastical buildings such as chapels and hermitages, the history of religious guilds, and changes in the objects of charitable bequests. However, this paper is concerned not with these subjects, but with religion, education, inheritance patterns and women.

The observations which I am about to make are based on three groups of wills: first, all the wills made between 1550 and 1640 by the inhabitants of a group of nine small parishes in or near the Waveney valley; second, those from 1550 to 1600 for the market town of Bungay on the Suffolk/Norfolk county boundary; and third, all the pre-1540 wills for two other parishes lying not far south of the first group. Only in the case of the first group have the Prerogative Court of Canterbury wills been used.

TABLE 1

Sources of Wills

	S. Elmham (9 parishes) 1550–1640	Bungay 1550–1600	Fressingfield & Laxfield 1372–1540
NCC[1]	78	53	60
AS[2]	192	74	127
PCC[3]	12	–	–
Total	282	127	187

[1] Norwich Consistory Court
[2] Archdeaconry of Suffolk
[3] Prerogative Court of Canterbury

There has been much discussion of what percentage of the population as a whole made wills and what proportion of the wills made has survived. It is impossible to arrive at accurate figures, but Table 2 is based on an attempt to arrive at a crude estimate of the percentage of the inhabitants of Flixton in South Elmham who made wills between 1560 and 1600. The calculation is based on the number of adult burials in the parish; children and wives have been omitted because neither group was likely to make will. It would have been instructive to have made a comparison with Bungay over the same forty-year period, but this was not possible as the burial registers of the two parishes in the town make no distinction between adults and children.

TABLE 2

	Flixton burials 1560–1600		Flixton wills 1560–1600
Adult males	42	Men	10 (24%)
Widows	28	Widows	1 (3.5%)

All the parishes mentioned above lie in the wood-pasture area of East Anglia, a region which was relatively wealthy in the early modern period and which supported a high density of small farms, many of whose owners also pursued a craft or trade. Dual occupations were extremely common in the wood-pasture district, so much so as to be almost the norm. Ever since at least the early fourteenth century wood-pasture Suffolk had been outstandingly rich. In 1334 this area was assessed at a figure higher than the average for the eastern counties,[1] and two centuries later it supported a large number of taxpayers paying a high rate of tax.[2] The wealth of the area was due both to the density of the population and to the high proportion of yeomen in Hoxne and Wangford hundreds, in which all these parishes are to be found. The presence of large numbers of yeomen can be taken as an indication that this was a wealthy area. Study of the circumstances of a number of these yeomen has shown that they were richer in many ways than their contemporaries in other less favoured regions of England. They tended to live in larger and better furnished houses, to own bigger herds of cattle, to possess more books and silver, and to make more generous provision for their widows and younger sons.[3]

It is not surprising to find that the religious preambles to pre-Reformation wills follow the standard form. Almost universal provision is made for a token payment for unpaid tithes to the high altar of the deceased's parish church. Again almost all testators make arrangements for the saying of masses for their souls, and legacies to the preaching orders of friars are common; the monastic

TABLE 3

Social status of testators

Social status	South Elmham		Bungay	
Gentlemen	12	4%	3	2%
Clergy	9	3%	4	7.5%
Yeomen	77	27%	8	6%
Husbandmen	18	6%	1	0.7%
Widows	55	19.5%	20	16%
Singlemen/women	9	3%	4	5%
Wives	1	0.3%	–	
Craftsmen/tradesmen	21	7%	38	30%
Labourers/servants	4	1%	–	
Unknown	81	28.5%	48	38%

The Fressingfield and Laxfield wills have been omitted from this table as few of them give status or occupation.

orders are seldom remembered in these wills. The arrangements made by testators for what they called the 'health' of their souls vary in complexity and are obviously dependent on the wealth of the individual. They range from a shilling or so to pay a priest to say a few masses to payments of ten pounds to enable a priest to travel to Rome to pray there for the departed's soul. Less than three percent of the pre-1540 wills provide for pilgrimages to Rome, but that Suffolk rural communities contained even a few people wealthy enough to make such bequests is another indication of the wealth of the area. Between the two extremes come arrangements of varying elaboration for the salvation of souls. Those who could not afford costly private arrangements made use of the services of the priest employed by their parish guild. Religious guilds were extremely common in medieval East Anglia and were to be found in most parishes. Both Fressingfield and Laxfield had a guild, and larger places often had more than one; there were seven in Beccles. Membership of the guilds was widespread and was open to both men and women. Some of these devotional guilds merely burnt a light before the image of their patron saint, but many maintained a side chapel in the parish church or a free-standing chapel in the graveyard; the former was the case at Fressingfield and the latter at Laxfield. Many of them possessed guild halls, a number of which were later used as poor houses or schools, and not a few of these still survive. The religious guilds not only served the purpose of spiritual insurance societies, but also fulfilled some of the functions of modern burial clubs and friendly societies. It is probable that in the late medieval period these guilds were the centre of most of the social activity in rural communities.

The earliest known reference to a guild in East Anglia is that to the guild of St Thomas the Martyr at Wymondham in Norfolk in 1187, and in general there are few records of guilds before the middle of the fourteenth century. Their proliferation in the fifteenth century grew from the stress laid by the late medieval church on the doctrine of purgatory and the resulting obsession with the salvation of souls. Many of the guilds accumulated considerable wealth, mainly from bequests made by their members. Fifteenth- and early sixteenth-century wills contain much information on these subjects, and gifts included land, houses, livestock and objects such as cooking pots. In Fressingfield almost all bequests to the parish guild took the form of cash, but in Laxfield it was much more usual to leave legacies in kind; there seems no reason for this difference between neighbouring and very similar parishes. Between 1465 and 1525 eight cows were left to Laxfield's guild of St Mary as well as various utensils and items of furniture. For instance in 1472 William Markaunt bequeathed it a brass cauldron, a pot, a large bowl, a table with two trestles and two benches, and a tablecloth.[4] The accumulation of funds allowed many guilds to build premises in which to hold feasts, keep their property and house the guild priest if one was employed. In Suffolk many of these guildhalls date from the first two decades of the sixteenth century and often replaced earlier and smaller buildings. Fressingfield built a new guildhall between 1500 and 1509, and Laxfield followed suit in the next decade; both these guildhalls still exist. There is some doubt as to the precise functions and activities for which the guildhalls were used, but this quotation from a document of 1509 concerning the newly built one at Fressingfield gives some idea of their purpose: the churchwardens and parishoners were to use the building 'for the kepyng of all church ales, Gildes, yerdayes, buryngges and other drynkyngges necessary to the p[ro]fyte of the seid chirch or p[ar]isshe', and it had been built 'for the more rev[er]ens of God and in avoydyng of etynge and drynkyng and other abusions in the chirch'.[5]

The later wills from the nine parishes of South Elmham and from Bungay show the usual change from pre- to post-Reformation preambles. The changes coincide so neatly with the various about-turns in religion between 1547 and 1559 that it is hard to believe that they always express deeply held beliefs. There are some curious hybrid preambles, dating mainly from Mary's reign, which read very much like those of convinced Calvinists with their expressions of belief in salvation through Christ's death and passion alone and in the testator's own membership of the elect who can expect to inherit the kingdom of heaven, but coupled with a plea for the intercession of the Virgin and Saints. What is one to make of these? Are they an attempt to be prepared for all eventualities, or do they result from theological confusion? In any case the study of wills drawn up by known will writers shows that scribes tended to use their own formulae, and so most religious preambles are not in the words of the testator, but at the same time it is unlikely that a man making a will would choose a scribe whose religious views were diametrically opposed to his own.[6]

Before leaving the subject of religion it seems worth considering whether Puritan or Calvinist beliefs were more common among urban than rural testators.

TABLE 4

Religious views expressed in wills

	Anglican		Puritan		Roman Catholic		Neutral		None	
South Elmham 1550–1640 (282 wills)	160	57%	20	7%	33	12%	12	4%	57	20%
Bungay 1550–1600 (127 wills)	47	37%	32	25%	16	12.5%	16	12.5%	16	12.5%

It is impossible to be absolutely certain about the precise significance of religious sentiments in preambles, but those classified as Puritan express the belief that the testator is one of the elect. Not surprisingly, with one exception, there are no Roman Catholic preambles after 1559. The odd one out was made in 1595 and is that of a gentleman who mentioned saints and angels. It is the nuncupative wills which lack preambles, and those in the group classified as non-committal are very brief and say no more than 'I bequeath my soul to almighty God'.

Table 4 shows that orthodox Anglican beliefs were far more frequently expressed by testators living in the rural parishes of South Elmham than by those dwelling in Bungay. This bears out the view that town-dwellers, and in particular craftsmen and tradesmen, were more likely to hold radical religious views. From Table 3 it can be seen that the percentage of wills made by this class in Bungay is over four times higher than in South Elmham. The presence of lecturers or preachers, in addition to the parish clergy, in towns is one reason for the higher incidence of Calvinist views there. There were several Puritan preachers in the district in the reign of Elizabeth I and one, who had been deprived of his living for refusal to conform, was certainly preaching in Bungay around 1600.[7] In several Bungay wills a sum of money is left to pay for the preaching of one or more sermons, and in one case this man was specifically named as the preacher of a funeral sermon.[8] Nearly half (40%) of the Bungay wills used for this paper were written by five men: three clergymen and two laymen. All those written by the former have preambles which can be classified as orthodox Anglican, while those drawn up by the other two men are consistently Puritan in tone; one of the two laymen was a draper. Even if the phrases used are those of the will writer rather than of the testator it must be assumed that the man chosen to draw up a will held religious views in agreement with those of the person whose will he was writing.

While pre-Reformation wills can be taken as a good guide to the pre-occupation of testators with the shortening of the term their souls would spend in purgatory, it would be unwise to place too much reliance on post-Reformation preambles as a guide to religious belief.

Dr Cressy[9] found a high rate of literacy in East Anglia, so it is surprising that only thirteen (2%) of the approximately 600 wills used in this paper make specific arrangements about the education of children. Even more unexpected is the absence of instructions about education from the Bungay wills. A grammar school was founded there in 1564, but only one Bungay testator refers to the education of his children. This man asked his wife to bring up their two sons virtuously and in learning until they were old enough to be apprenticed. Yet at least thirty-four (27%) of the Bungay testators left under-age children. References to the upbringing of children are found in almost all these wills, and in several cases instructions are left for the apprenticing of sons and daughters. However, there are three wills, two of which are those of masters of the grammar school, which make substantial bequests for the support of poor scholars at Bungay grammar school.

In seven (5.5%) of the Bungay wills books are mentioned; only a bible in all except two cases. One of the schoolmasters lists a considerable number of books, but the other man to bequeath more than a bible was a tailor who possessed a book of common prayer, a book entitled 'the ymage of god' and other unnamed books, some of which he bequeathed to the clergyman who wrote his will.

The pre-1540 wills from Fressingfield and Laxfield produced seven (4%) specific statements about the education of sons. Simon Jurdon, who died in 1471, left his wife the income from his land and tenements to be used in part to 'find his seven sons to school or to good guidance'.[10] One man asked that his son should go to grammar school until he was twenty-one, which seems a remarkably late age; another wished his children to be brought up at home until seven years old and then sent to school or placed in service as his executors thought best. In 1445 six shillings and eight pence a year was apparently enough to pay for a boy's schooling, and in 1519 a bequest was made to enable a grandson to be 'found to school till he can write a man's name and read it.'[11] This implies no more than basic schooling. In another will it is interesting to find that only the youngest of three sons was to be sent to school, and for three years only; his two elder brothers had both been left land. It seems likely that this testator felt that education would be of use to a landless boy, but was not needed by his elder brothers. There are similar cases amongst the South Elmham wills.

If more of the wills used had been made by men with young sons, it is possible that a higher percentage would have included provision for the education of children. It is difficult to know what significance, if any, to attach to the absence of reference to the local grammar school in Bungay wills, but it was not unreasonable to expect to find more bequests concerning education in a place where a school was known to exist. The early records of this school were destroyed in a fire in 1688 so it is not possible to check whether any of the testators or their sons were amongst its pupils.

The pattern of inheritance is both determined by economic circumstances and has an important effect on them. In a wealthy area, such as wood-pasture Suffolk, it is not surprising to find a considerable number of men rich enough to set up more than one son with land. It is generally held that partible inheritance was fairly widespread in East Anglia, but what is being considered here is not the subdivision of the family holding between two or more sons, but the acquisition of land specifically for the purpose of providing farms for younger sons. It is often clearly stated in wills that the land left to the younger sons has been recently bought by the testator.

TABLE 5

Types of bequests in wills

	Land/houses		*Cash*[1]		*Number of men leaving widows*	
pre-1540 187 wills	84	45%	70	37%	93	50%
Bungay 127 wills	73	57%	50	39%	76	60%

[1] Cash bequests to wives and children only; charitable and other cash legacies excluded.

Table 5 covers two types of legacies made to wives and children in the pre-1540 wills from two rural parishes and in thc group of urban wills belonging to the second half of the sixteenth century. The ten percent increase in bequests of real estate in the later wills may well be insignificant. In theory there was no need to make testamentary dispositions of copyhold land as its descent was governed by manorial custom, but in practice it seems to have become much more common for testators to make such arrangements after the middle of the sixteenth century. This may in part have been due to a decrease in manorial control in a region which was never strongly manorialized and where copyhold of inheritance was the normal form of unfree tenure.

The absence of all reference to land in a will cannot be taken to imply that the testator was landless. He may have relied on the workings of manorial custom, or have already made over his land to adult sons. Other sources show that in the wood–pasture district of East Anglia it was by no means the rule for marriage to be delayed until after the death of the father, and indeed many of the wills refer to married sons and grandchildren. It is an indication of the close involvement of town dwellers with the surrounding countryside that it was just as common for Bungay men to leave land as it was for those in the two rural parishes.

TABLE 6

Bequests of land

1   *Before 1540* (Fressingfield & Laxfield)

a)[1]

To widow for life/term of years and then to son	41	59%
To widow absolutely	6	8.5%
To widow and son jointly	2	3%
To childless widow for life	10	14.5%

b)[2]

To one son who had brothers	12	14%
To only son	20	24%
To more than one son	16	19%
To a daughter whose brothers also left land	2	2%

[1] percentages in (a) are of 69 wills made by men whose wives were living and who left land/houses.
[2] percentages in (b) are of 84 wills in which bequests were made of land/houses.

2   *Bungay 1550–1600*

a)[1]

To widow for life/term of years and then to son	40	62.5%
To widow absolutely	13	20%
To widow and son jointly	1	1.5%
To childless widow for life	6	9%

b)[2]

To one son who had brothers	7	9.5%
To only son	6	8%
To more than one son	15	20.5%
To daughter whose brothers also left land	5	7%

[1] percentages in (a) are of 64 wills made by men whose wives were living and who left land/houses.
[2] percentages in (b) are of 73 wills in which bequests were made of land/houses.

In Table 6 bequests of houses and land to widows and children have been broken down for the same two groups of wills as were used for Table 5. There seems to be little difference between the way real estate was disposed of by the two groups of testators. The increase in the later period of almost twelve percent in the number of widows who were left land absolutely is partly compensated for by the accompanying fall in the bequests of land for life to childless widows; another factor must be the higher percentage of Bungay men whose wives survived them.

The most interesting features of this table are the high percentage of bequests of land to a widow for her lifetime or until the inheriting son attains the age of majority; the latter is far less common than the former; and the ability of a fifth of testators to set up more than one son with a farm. In practice it is probable that many widows handed over their land to adult sons, but the presence of livestock, dairy utensils and implements of husbandry in widows' wills shows that this did not always happen. It is surely an illustration of the wealth of many testators that they were able to make such provision for two or more sons; occasionally as many as four or five sons are left some land.

Of course wills only tell us what the testators intended to happen. The death of one or more sons must often have overset testamentary arrangements and in fact many wills include complicated provisions for just this eventuality. In practice this means that in some cases one son inherited property intended for several. To arrive at a true picture of what really happened to the land bequeathed in these wills could only be achieved by using other documentary sources, such as parish registers and manorial records, together with the wills. Although Table 6 must be taken as illustrating a hypothetical rather than a real pattern of land inheritance, this does not alter the fact that we are considering a group which included a large proportion of wealthy testators.

It has been suggested that efforts to establish younger sons with farms led to a weakening of the original family holding and to the setting-up of new holdings too small to be viable.[12] This may well have been the case in open-field areas, but in wood-pasture East Anglia the viability of small farms was made possible by the combination of by-industry with highly profitable dairy farming. Furthermore, as has already been pointed out, most of the testators who left land to more than one son were not sub-dividing a holding, but had bought more land specifically for the purpose of providing younger sons with holdings.

TABLE 7

Cash bequests

	Fressingfield & Laxfield before 1540		Bungay 1550–1600	
Landless children	32	17%	19	15%
Landless wife	15	8%	5	4%
All children	11	6%	8	6%
Daughters only	10	5%	12	9.5%

Turning to cash legacies, Table 7 shows their distribution amongst different types of recipient. So many testators either left only one son or provided land for more than one that cash legacies appear considerably less frequently in wills than do those of land. It was more usual for cash legacies to be paid to his siblings by the son who inherited his father's land than for them to be taken directly out of the deceased's estate. Often these payments were spread over a period of years, and in some cases must have proved a considerable drain on the income of the inheriting son. However, the fact that this type of arrangement was so common suggests that it cannot have been a frequent cause of bankruptcy, and that many testators believed their farms to be capable of providing an income adequate for supporting these payments. Careful research into the history of holdings thus burdened with payments of portions is needed before any firm conclusions can be drawn about the effect of this kind of legacy. It would also be interesting to know how often payments were delayed because of the effects of bad havests or of a fall in the prices of agricultural produce. Here again dairy farmers were probably better placed than their contemporaries in arable farming districts.

Table 8 shows the frequency of bequests in cash and kind to landless children. Dr Howell has suggested that an increase in cash legacies at the expense of those in kind is an indication of growing prosperity.[13] In south-east Leicestershire there were far fewer portions in kind after 1560 than there had been earlier, but in north-east Suffolk there seems little difference between the two groups of wills. If Dr Howell's thesis is correct, this must mean that East Anglian farmers had achieved a level of prosperity in the late middle ages and early Tudor period that was not to be attained in

TABLE 8

Legacies in cash and kind

		Cash	Kind	Both
Before 1540	*Sons*	46%	6.5%	8%
	Daughters	59%	8%	10%
Bungay 1550–1600	*Sons*	43%	6.5%	13%
	Daughters	61%	2%	19.5%

The percentages are of the number of wills which make bequests of cash, goods or livestock to children who did not receive land.

Leicestershire until the reign of Elizabeth I. There seems no reason to doubt that legacies in cash rather than in kind are an indication of increasing prosperity. They must indicate the ability of testators to provide portions for daughters and younger sons without the need to divide up the family's moveable property. In Leicestershire portions in kind were fifty percent of the total in the period 1560 to 1640, but in Suffolk they were never anywhere near that level even in the fifteenth century. This is not surprising in view of the fact that wood-pasture Suffolk lies in the region that was the most economically advanced in England throughout the middle ages and early modern period.

What did the recipients do with their cash legacies? In the case of girls they provided marriage portions, but some sons may have been in a position to buy land. Many boys must have used their legacies to finance an apprenticeship or to set themselves up in trade. In a period when many new industries were emerging, and the numerous market towns of East Anglia were growing, there must have been ample opportunities for young men with some capital to make their way. Thus, as Dr Howell has suggested, profitable farming generated recruits for the new urban middle class. Her other point, that the giving of legacies in cash helped to preserve farms from endless sub-division,[14] serves to explain the continuing prosperity of small-scale farming in wood-pasture East Anglia and the adoption there of advanced agricultural methods, such as ley farming and turnip growing.

Wills are the best available source for a large scale study of inheritance patterns, but, bearing in mind that they represent

ntions and not what actually happened, they must be
caution. Ideally inheritance should be investigated by
demographic evidence and that from manor court rolls
information provided by wills. Another problem arising
use of wills is the possibility that will-making is an atypical
[5] The only answer to this difficulty seems to be more surveys
of w.. made wills, why they did so and what proportion of the adult
population they represent.

Alice Clark's *Working Life of Women in the Seventeenth Century*
suggested the idea of looking in wills for indications of the social and
economic position of women. Legally their position was extremely
weak and this is illustrated by the bequests some men made to their
wives of the household goods that had been their property before
marriage. In some cases women were even left their own clothes. In
practice, however, women seemed to have played a far more active
part in the economy that their legal position would suggest.

TABLE 9

Women as executors of wills

	No of Testators leaving a widow	Sole executrix		Joint executor	
Fressingfield	44	1	2%	14	32%
Laxfield	53	7	13%	23	43%
Bungay	83	41	49%	20	24%
South Elmham	163	57	35%	46	28%

In the first place women were frequently appointed as executors
of their husbands' wills, and many of them were the sole executrix.
Table 9 shows the frequency of women executors, and indicates that
women not only fulfilled this role more frequently after 1550 than
before, but also were more often the sole executrix in the later
period. The very high level of female executors in Bungay may show
that, as Alice Clark suggests, women in the early modern period
took an active part in the running of their husbands' businesses and
were thus well qualified to wind up their affairs or to continue to run
the family shop. It was not unheard of for women to manage a shop.
Several widows in the wills used for this paper were left a shop
absolutely or for life, and the records of Beccles market in the
seventeenth century show women as stall holders.

Many testators expressed their confidence and trust in their wives as executors in terms such as this: 'my special truste and confidence is in her'.[16] Some men stipulated that their wives must not damage property left to them for life on pain of losing the bequest, but such statements are the exception rather than the rule. There is little evidence of the lack of affection between spouses believed by Stone to be the normal state of affairs before the late seventeenth century.[17] It is also far more usual for a wife to be left property for life than for her widowhood only.

The great majority of men whose wives survived them left them either all their moveable property or the unbequeathed residue thereof. These bequests of household goods and livestock were generally unconditional, and this freedom to do what they wished with moveables may explain the large numbers of widows' wills. The wills of widows are usually concerned solely with the disposal of goods and cash. Table 10 is based on a sample of all wills proved in the Norwich Consistory Court between 1560 and 1686.

TABLE 10

Widows' wills as a percentage of all wills

1560–1603	17%
1604–1686	13%

Alice Clark's thesis that the economic position of women seriously declined after about 1660 may explain the lower percentage of widows' wills in the seventeenth century. Widows also made fewer wills in the pre-1540 period: only twenty-two (12%) of the 187 Fressingfield and Laxfield wills used were those of widows. Sixteen percent of Bungay and seventeen and a half percent of the South Elmham wills are those of widows, and, if wills made by people of unknown status are omitted, a quarter of the wills made by inhabitants of both places were made by widows.

Why were widows such a substantial will-making group? An analysis of the wills of the fifty-five South Elmham widows whose wills were proved between 1550 and 1640 suggested that the main reason why a widow made a will was to dispose of her personal property, which was usually inherited from her husband. Two other pressing reasons for making a will were the existence of under-age children or childlessness. Five of the South Elmham widows were leaving young children, and nearly a quarter of their number had no children living. It seems safe to regard these three reasons as the motives governing the making of wills by widows. Any community with a number of male testators able to make ample provision for their wives is likely also to contain a high percentage of will-making widows.

TABLE 11

Bequests made by South Elmham widows

Type of bequest	Number	Percentage[1]
Land	9	16
Cows	17	31
Cows & other livestock	7	13
Cash	41	74.5
Furniture	39	71
Utensils	28	51
Valuables	14	25
Clothes	26	47
Linen	23	42
Books	2	4

[1] Percentage of 55 widows' wills.

There is no doubt that the South Elmham widows were a wealthy group. The sums left in cash legacies range from 6s 8d to £254 18s 4d. Table 12 shows the distribution by value of cash bequests, and that nearly half of them were worth twenty pounds or more.

TABLE 12

Cash legacies by South Elmham widows

Under £1	£1–£9	£10–£19	£20–£99	Over £100
2	14	5	16	4
5%	34%	12%	39%	10%

The percentages are of the 41 wills with cash legacies.

Table 13 illustrates that the wealth of South Elmham widows lay in goods as well as money, and that many of them were actively engaged in farming.

TABLE 13

Cows and calves left by 17 widows

4 or less	5–9	10–19	20 or more
5	4	6	2
29%	23.5%	35%	12%

Evidence about the economic and social status of women is scattered amongst a wide variety of documents and is not always easily discovered, but the analysis presented above shows that wills are a valuable source for the lives of women in the past.

There is no doubt that wills are one of the most important sources for economic and social historians of early modern society. They provide a wide variety of information, and give a better insight into both the material and spiritual circumstances of men's lives than do most other classes of documents. When used in conjunction with other sources they can do much to widen our knowledge of the past.

Notes

1 R.E. Glasscock, 'The Distribution of Wealth in East Anglia in the early fourteenth century', *Transactions of the Institute of British Geographers*, 32 (1963), p.115

2 J. Sheail, 'The Distribution of Taxable Population and Wealth in England during the early Sixteenth Century', *Transactions of the Institute of British Geographers, 55 (1972), pp. 117–119.*

3 N. Evans, 'The Community of South Elmham, Suffolk 1550–1640', (unpublished University of East Anglia M. Phil. thesis, 1978), passim.

4 Suffolk Record Office, Ipswich (henceforth SRO) IC/AA2/2/244.

5 SRO, FC90/L3/8 Deed dated 20 February 1509.

6 Margaret Spufford, 'The Scribes of Villagers' Wills in the sixteenth and seventeenth centuries and their influence', *Local Population Studies*,7, (Autumn 1971), p.41 and N.R. Evans, 'Testators, Literacy, Education and Religious Belief', forthcoming article in *Local Population Studies*.

7 Norfolk Record Office (henceforth NRO), DEP 32, pp.347–8.

8   NRO, Norwich Consistory Court 10 Chandler, Will of John Dowsinge the elder.

9   D.A. Cressy, 'Education and Literacy in London and East Anglia 1580–1700', unpublished Cambridge Ph.D. thesis, 1972.

10 SRO, ICAA2/2/309 Will of Simon Jurdon of Laxfield.

11 SRO, ICAA2/8/60 Will of John Cowper of Laxfield.

12 Margaret Spufford, 'Peasant inheritance customs and land distribution in Cambridgeshire from the sixteenth to the eighteenth century', in Jack Goody, Joan Thirsk and E.P. Thompson (eds), *Family and Inheritance: Rural Society in Western Europe 1200–1800*, (Cambridge, 1976), pp.166–7 (henceforth Spufford).

13 Cicely Howell, 'Peasant inheritance customs in the Midlands 1280–1700', in Jack Goody, Joan Thirsk and E.P. Thompson (eds), *Family and Inheritance: Rural Society in Western Europe 1200–1800*, (Cambridge, 1976), pp.151–2 (henceforth Howell).

14 Howell, p.153.

15 Spufford, p.176 and N.R. Evans, 'Testators, Literacy, Education and Religious Belief', forthcoming article in *Local Population Studies*.

16 NRO, Norwich Consistory Court 24 Lyncolne. Will of Richard Lessye, 1552.

17 L. Stone, *Family, Sex and Marriage in England 1500–1800*, 1978, passim.

WILLS AND THE COMMUNITY:
A CASE STUDY OF TUDOR GRANTHAM

Stephen Coppel

In recent years wills and inventories have aroused considerable interest among historians of the early modern period. Deposited in archival repositories throughout England, these records constitute a major source for historians. The research possibilities of probate records would appear to be manifold. Already they have been culled by historians engaged in fields as diverse as demography, family and inheritance, land economy, popular religion and charity, education, cultural life and domestic achitecture. Wills and inventories have also demonstrated their value in the study of past communities best exemplified perhaps in Margaret Spufford's *Contrasting Communities*.[1] It is here at the level of local history that probate records appear to me to offer their greatest potential. They permit the local historian armed with other sources to reconstruct partially the willmaking class, obtaining thereby some idea of their activities and attitudes and of the family and community ties operating in the locality. The context of the local community affords a suitable framework for examining the willmaking process in detail, especially the formulation and witnessing of wills, the personal disposition of property and bequests, and the appointment of legal deputies to execute the testator's last will. It is with these purposes in mind that I am at present engaged in a special study of willmaking in the Lincolnshire town of Grantham in the sixteenth century. It is later projected to contrast the urban case of Grantham with the marshland agricultural community of Leverton and thus to assess to what extent local forces and customs shaped willmaking behaviour. As it is still premature to draw significant conclusions from my data, my intention here is to present rather a methodological discussion, to provide those of you who may be less familiar with wills with some idea of the nature of this source and of the sorts of questions that may be asked of it. I wish furthermore to elucidate some of the problems inherent in wills and to demonstrate how some of these may be confronted and partly resolved by referring to examples from my own research in the community of Grantham.

The will, according to a legal definition, is the documentary instrument by which a person regulates the rights of others to his property or family after his death.[2] In the sixteenth century the testator usually referred to the document as 'my last will and testament'. The will and testament by strict definition were two separate instruments, and at least during the early part of the century this distinction seems to have been observed. The will is concerned with the disposition of realty (lands and tenements); it took legal effect not by an act of probate, which in respect of land the church courts were not empowered to grant, but by virtue of the will's signature. The testament is concerned with the disposition of personal goods (furniture, clothing, livestock, tools of trade or agriculture, cash and debts) and the grant of probate by the church courts applied to this alone. For the sake of convenience, however, the two instruments were included under one document, the 'last will' sometimes appearing as a separate section within it.[3] In this paper, the term 'will' is used to signify the one document containing the disposition of both real property and personal goods.

What could be disposed by will? Prior to 1540 it was illegal to devise by will lands held by descent, although it was legally permissible to devise purchased lands or lands held by lease. To circumvent these restrictions, it was general practice to devise land by 'uses', a legal devise which distinguished title to land from its enjoyment. By this method land was conveyed in the testator's lifetime to trustees, or feoffees to uses, who then held it to his use. In this way, the testator could dispose his land by directing the feoffees to devise it according to the terms of his last will. The Grantham willmaker John Sleford provides an illustration of these practices in his will of 1525. The yeoman willed to his wife for the term of her widowhood, 'all my landes purchased and all my leases', after which they were to pass to his son and his heirs. But should mother and son for some reason fail to agree, the son was to enter all his father's lands in the nearby parish of Great Ponton. The willmaker concluded his will with the usual instruction, 'yt my feoffes stand feoffed and be seased of and in all my said landes & tenementes to the use and performans of this my last will'.[4] By means of the use the disposition of land by will had become common practice by the early sixteenth century. In 1526 the Statute of Uses attempted to put an end to it by prohibiting all further devises of land by will. However the confusion this created led to the enactment of the Statute of Wills in 1540 which finally legalized the disposition by written will of any lands held in fee simple.[5]

Not everyone was entitled to make a will. As a rule a will of land in the sixteenth century could not be made by those under the age of twenty-one, married women, excommunicants, or those of unsound mind.[6] A will made by a woman before marriage was declared void on matrimony while one made during marriage remained void even if she survived her husband. These restrictions could be overcome in certain circumstances by a settlement before marriage where the husband permitted his wife to make a will of personal goods up to a specific value or a will of land that had been reserved to her enjoyment. But in the town of Grantham at least no such wills of married women are to be found.

For a will to be declared valid, it was necessary for a minimum of two persons to witness the publication and sealing of the will in the presence of the testator. However, if there was proof that the will had been written in the testator's own hand, no witnesses were required.[7] Witnesses were usually friends and family members, often with the scribe and parish vicar as well; on some occasions the witness was a stranger. An example of the witnessing of wills is found in the case of the Lincolnshire widow Elizabeth Clarke of Tattershall who had her will attested in 1564 by two labourers unknown to her. According to their disposition before the church court, the two men

> '[were] bringing a barrell of bere from Tattershall unto billingaie [Billinghay] upon a Thursdaie about a fortnight before our ladie daie last and as thei were at Tattershall Ferie laboring to sett the same into a bote, thei were called into the house of the said Elizabeth Clarke the same daie being about iij of the clocke at afternoone to bere witnes of her will and when thei came in one John Bones of Tattershall did rede the will here exhibited wch so being redd the said Elizabeth Clarke did approve to be her will leing then sicke in hir parlor'.[8]

Every will required the nomination of an executor. If no executor was named and there were no grounds for assuming that the residuary legatee had been intended, the willmaker was deemed to have died as an intestate, and an administration with the will annexed was committed to the widow or next of kin who then settled the estate.[9] After the willmaker's decease, the executor who intended to act received custody of the deceased's goods, arranged for his burial, supervised the taking of an inventory and the appraisal of his goods, and then presented the will and often the inventory with it to the appropriate church court of probate. Once the will had been approved, the executor discharged the debts, funeral expenses and legacies from the estate and finally rendered an account of his actions to the court.[10]

The historian who decides to use wills therefore must be aware of the basic legal requirements of willmaking and the procedure for obtaining probate and executing the will. As a source, the historian must recognize that the will is inherently inclined towards the older, male and propertied sections of the community. Prior allocations of goods and earlier settlements of land are a further problem, frustrating any study of inheritance patterns from wills alone. Nevertheless the disposition of property by wills is in itself of great interest, especially in the study of provision for family dependents whether unmarried, under age or in widowhood. Furthermore, it should be remembered that wills were usually written at the end of the testator's life, at a time when the willmaker was labouring under mortal illness and faced with the prospect of imminent death. Hence whatever the will reveals about attitudes, beliefs and intentions must somewhat be influenced by the condition of the willmaker and the circumstances of its formulation.

It is with these problems in mind that I now turn to the willmaking community of Grantham. The town is located in the southwestern corner of the county, lying in a valley below the limestone heath that runs to the north. In the sixteenth century Grantham was a small-scale urban community. The ecclesiastical census of 1563 recorded 252 households in the town and its total population can be surmised at just over 1,000.[11] But its small size belies the importance of the town. The Great North road passed close to it, providing custom and exchange for the community and by 1464 the town had become incorporated by royal charter. Political control was invested in an oligarchy of twelve life-tenured comburgesses while the town's alderman was elected annually from their number. The twelve were also the justices of the peace whose jurisdictional authority extended over the soke of Grantham – an area of special jurisdiction enjoyed by the town over several villages and hamlets in the locality. The parish church was the spiritual focus of the town, its soaring steeple a testimony to civic pride and late medieval prosperity.[12] The demography of the town in the sixteenth century (Figure 1) suggests a buoyant upward movement during the later

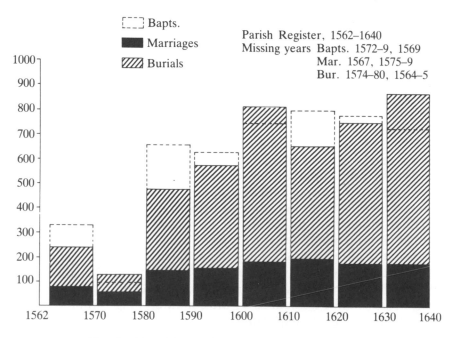

Fig. 1   Grantham Demographic Profile, 1562–1640

part of the century. The first eighty years of the parish register extant from 1562 have been plotted in ten year totals, with the missing years of the register accounting for the drop in the 1570's. The Grantham demographic profile is characterized by births rising slightly above deaths, except in years of plague, 1604 and 1637. At the end of the former year 1604/5, the parish clerk remarked in the register: 'buried this yeare of all diseases 327', a year of crisis mortality that depleted the town's population by perhaps as much as a quarter.[13] Nevertheless, natural increase within the next decade

seems to have restored the demographic stability of the town until
the next outbreak of plague.

TABLE 1

Probate Records of Grantham, 1501–1600

Period	Burials	W	WI	Total W	Adm	Adm Acc	AdmI	Total Adm	I	Total I
1501–10	–	2	–	2	–	–	–	–	1	1
1511–20	–	–	–	–	–	–	–	–	–	–
1521–30	–	6	–	6	–	–	–	–	–	–
1531–40	–	14	3	17	–	–	–	–	–	3
1541–50	–	4	7	11	–	–	–	–	4	11
1551–60	–	12	16	28	–	–	–	–	11	27
1561–70	244	5	7	12	5	1	4	9	2	13
1571–80	133[1]	6	21	27	3	1	–	3	4	25
1581–90	477	8	15	23	5	2	9	14	–	24
1591–1600	581	3	22	25	8	8	20	28	–	42
Total	1435	60	91	151	21	12	33	54	22	146

[1] Parish register, missing years 1574–80

W = Will
I = Inventory
Adm = Administration
Acc = Account

The probate records for Grantham are listed in Table 1 and all are
deposited in the Lincolnshire Archives office, with the exception of
nine Prerogative Court of Canterbury wills at the Public Record
Office. There are 151 wills surviving for Grantham in the sixteenth
century and all except the nine are Lincoln archdeaconry wills.
Probate in the archdeaconry wills was usually granted by a court
deputy holding the combined office of archdeacon's official and
bishop's commissary; the archdeacon himself rarely presided in
person at probate.[14] The wills were proved either at Lincoln or in the
Grantham locality within the course of a regular church court
circuit. About half the wills were brought the distance of 25 miles to
Lincoln, an undertaking which appears to have had its merit in a
swifter grant of probate. Probate was granted with relative speed,
68% of wills being proved within two months of burial (see Table 5)
– a finding corroborated in recent work by R. Houlbrooke for

Norwich Consistory Court and two archdeaconry courts.[15] Probate could be granted within a matter of days: Robert Gregge obtained probate at Lincoln within three days of his burial, the innkeeper Christopher Lupton within four and the glover Richard Primette within five.[16] In nine cases the executor, or his proxy, was required to travel further afield to obtain probate at the Prerogative Court of Canterbury in London, the highest court of probate in the realm. These were Lincolnshire willmakers who in theory possessed moveable goods of over £10 in more than one diocese, although in my sample, these were located not in another diocese but in a different archdeaconry within the diocese.[17] The grant of probate in the PCC wills was much slower taking an average of two months, although the baker William Smyth secured probate within a record five days of his burial.[18]

It will be seen from Table 1 that probate records survive in larger numbers from the second half of the sixteenth century. Moreover there is a higher chance of finding a will and an inventory relating to the same testator towards the end of the period. The paucity of earlier records may partly be explained by poor survival and a less efficient system of record keeping. Nevertheless, there is evidence of increased willmaking in the later sixteenth century. A perusal of the probate registers in which the wills were entered reveals an unprecedented rise in the granting of probate in the latter half of the sixteenth century. This is observed across the county and indeed would seem to be the general experience in England. In the diocese of York, R.A. Marchant has shown that in the period 1500–1550 there was an annual average of 290 wills probated and 50 administrations issued, while in the early seventeenth century between 1612–1619 the corresponding averages record 970 probates and 675 administrations per annum. Marchant briefly attributes this increased volume of testamentary business to the circulation of 'more wealth in more hands' in the late sixteenth century following the dissolution of church properties and the rise in trade and industry.[19] For my part, I cannot offer with any certainty an adequate explanation why willmaking should be increasing on such a scale. It may have been due to a rise in real wealth; or simply that with rising inflation from 1540's more people had sufficient goods in value to warrant the formulation of a will. At any rate, one would expect to find greater participation in willmaking among the lower socio-economic classes and to some extent the Grantham evidence supports this. In Table 3, the wealth structure of willmakers is given based on the value of moveable goods appraised in complete inventories or recorded in the Probate Act book. It is found that 12% of willmakers, most of whom appear in the late sixteenth century, possessed moveable property of less than £5. Although willmaking was largely concentrated amongst the middling rich (those of appraised wealth between £20 and £100), the Grantham evidence does suggest that this activity had filtered down to the lower socio-economic levels of the community; a trend which would indicate that willmaking by the late sixteenth century was becoming a socially downward process.

TABLE 2

Proportion of willmakers and intestates to the dying adult population

Period	Burials	Adult Burials	W	(%)	Adm	(%)
1581–90	477	197	24	(12%)	14	(7%)
1591–1600	581	217	26	(12%)	28	(13%)
1601–1610	821	395	29	(7%)	46	(12%)
Total	1879	809	79	(10%)	88	(11%)

What proportion of the community do willmakers represent? Various estimates have been suggested in answer to this vexed question. In her preliminary findings for the Essex parish of Earls Colne, Sarah Harrison found only 8% of the dying adult population making a will between 1610–40. However, in the Cumbrian parish of Kirkby Lonsdale, it was found that within one chapelry one-third made a will, the Quakers representing the largest group and thereby possibly accounting for this high proportion.[20] In Table 2 I have attempted to provide an estimate of the proportion of Grantham willmakers to the dying adult population. The Grantham parish register mentions the deceased's marital status in the case of women while 'son of' or 'daughter of' has been taken to indicate the burial of a minor. Consequently the column headed 'Adult burials' denotes all those who legally could have made a will before death, that is, males over 21, widows and unmarried women. Over the thirty year period, 1581–1610, the average proportion of Grantham willmakers to the dying adult population appears to be 10%. The drop in proportion for the decade 1601–10 is accounted by the high mortality of the 1604 epidemic. In this year only three wills were made while fourteen administrations for intestates were issued, the highest number throughout the thirty year period. It is interesting to observe that while only 10% of the dying adult population made wills, an equally low percentage of those dying intestate received administrations for the settlement of their estates. It must be remembered therefore that the proportion of the community represented by probate records remains small.

TABLE 3

Wealth structure of willmakers, 1501–1600
(based on complete Inv.'s and Probate Act Book).

less than £5	11	(12%)
£5 up to £10	7	(7%)
£10 up to £20	17	(18%)
£20 up to £50	22	(23%)
£50 up to £100	20	(21%)
£100 up to £200	14	(15%)
£200 up to £500	2	(2%)
over £500	1	(1%)
Total	94	

Furthermore one needs to consider how typical of the community were willmakers and their wealth. The wealth structure of Grantham willmakers has been tabulated in Table 3 based on the value of their moveable property alone. The aparent bell curve is dominated by the middling rich who form 44% of the willmakers and who possessed moveable goods valued between £20 and £100. Willmakers range from the yeoman William Bland whose goods comprised only the clothes he wore valued at £1 to the woolmerchant Thomas Russell whose moveable property was worth over £1,000.[21] A study of the community based on wills, therefore, unavoidably creates certain distortions. As Gloria Main has reminded us, probate records raise the apparent level of wealth in the community and at the same time conceal the poorer and more numerous section of the community.[22]

The circumstances of will formulation also imposes on the source a measure of distortion. The will was generally drafted at the first sign of approaching death. Half of the Grantham willmakers whose dates of burial are known (see Table 4) made their wills within one week of death. Furthermore, of the 97 willmakers in Grantham who expressed their state of health, 96% noted that they were sick of body. The Grantham carpenter Harry Scot died on the same day that he made his will, while Robert Gregge ordered his will on the day his wife was buried, following her into the grave less than a week later.[23] The will therefore was the testator's ultimate public act representing the final conscious statement of his intentions prior to decease. In some ways, as Aries has suggested, it was part of the ritual preparation for death.[24] The proximity of death sometimes prompted deathbed penitence, anxiety for proper burial, or hasty provision for surviving dependents. The Grantham willmaker Matthew Peyke made his will while 'laboring in Extreme Sicknes' and his pitiful condition aroused the request for the consolation of burial, 'in such Catholique Solemnitye as the Charite of myne Executris shall beste provide'.[25] John Richardson lying on his death bed only had time to recommend his soul to almighty god, the virgin Mary and the saints and to leave his children and all his worldly belongings in the hands of his sister.[26] Sometimes no scribe was at hand and the willmaker died uttering an oral, or nuncupative, declaration of his will to those gathered about the sick chamber. In the case of Jane Clark, a single woman from the Lincolnshire village of Owersby, the vicar had almost finished writing down her will when her condition suddenly worsened and he hurried over to administer the last rites before she died. After her decease, he resumed his pen and completed the will according to her final uttered words.[27]

TABLE 4

Interval between willmaking and burial, 1562–1600

less than 1 week	24
1 week up to 2 weeks	7
2 weeks up to 3 weeks	2
3 weeks up to 4 weeks	3
1 month up to 3 months	3
3 months up to 6 months	1
6 months up to 1 year	2
over 5 years	5
	1
	—
	48

Who wrote wills and to what extent did those responsible contribute to or influence their final expression? The question of will authorship is of some importance particularly where the mental life of the willmaker is sought since it is not always certain that the attitudes and intentions expressed in the will were those of the testator.[28] Testamentary disputes in the church courts often involved cases of alleged manipulation of the testator whose weak physical condition made it difficult to ignore the advice of the scribe or to resist the pressure of importunate relatives gathered around the deathbed. It was to refute allegations of such malpractices that the vicar of Kirton in Holland wrote to the probate registrar at Lincoln in October 1567.

> 'These are to advertise [to] youe yᵗ my neighboure Marione Alben late of yⁱˢ towne of Kirton about the third day of yⁱˢ monethe did send for me to write hir will And althoghe at my first commynge to hir she was willinge wᵗ out further incumbrance of writinge yᵗ hir goodes should be equally divided amonges her iij children: yeat whan John Alben hir sonne, said, mother it will brede angre amonges us oneles ye apoynte our partes in writinge severally to be sett furthe, And by the advises of the said John e of other hir frendes yᵉʳ present (for who beinge witty will not give eare to yᵉ good counsell of tryed frendes) she was contented e well willinge afore my departure thence, to declare e did conclude her will as it is nowe penned by myne owne hand. And yⁱˢ I specyally noted, when she was makinge hir bequestes, John Alben hir sonne aforesaid althoghe he was assynged to be hir sole executoure did never yᵉ lesse desyre hir to geve sondry thinges to others, cravinge nothinge to hym self nor to any of his, whiche made me thinke yᵗ this former advise tended rayther to a quyetnes yᵉⁿ to his owne gayne. . .'[29]

This case typifies the sort of pressure and influence exerted by family and friends upon the willmaker during the formulation of the will. It also underlines the difficulty in knowing the origin of the personal attitudes and intentions contained in the will. This is particularly the case where religious attitudes are expressed in preambles for it is not clear if this is simply a conventional legal formula written by the scribe or a representation of the testator's religious opinions.

The Grantham evidence permits only a partial answer to these tantalizing problems of will authorship and influence. From the mid-sixteenth century the Grantham wills often mention the scribe responsible. About a dozen scribes can be identified, although only three or four wrote or witnessed wills in any number. The scribes were either local yeoman or vicars of the parish. The most prominent willwriters were the Wallis family who appear to have made it something of a family practice. James Wallis, a merchant of the Staple, penned his own will during a visit to London at a period when he was enjoying good health.[30] He was often present as a witness to wills and as an appraiser of inventories, although there is no firm evidence that he had acted as a scribe. It was his sons, Robert and John Wallis, who undertook willwriting as an occasional responsibility. Robert Wallis was called upon to write the wills of a dying bachelor and of an unmarried woman; both were accorded the standard preamble of justification by faith. Robert himself died soon after in 1595 without making a will.[31]

TABLE 5

Interval between burial and probate, 1581–1600

less than 2 months	32	(68%)
less than 1 year	13	(28%)
over 1 year	2	(4%)

His brother, the yeoman John Wallis, was the most prolific scrivener in Grantham, appearing as 'scripter' in a dozen wills within a space of fifteen years from 1588 to 1603. Some of the more influential and affluent willmakers in the community numbered among his clients. These included a glover, a saddler and two comburgesses all of whom left goods valued above £100.[32] John Wallis first appeared as a scribe in 1588 in the will of John Brotherton, a prosperous glover and former alderman of Grantham. The will committed the testator's soul into the hands of almighty god, trusting that it would be received through the merits of Christ's passion – a standard formula of justification by faith which John Wallis employed with occasional modifications during his years of activity. The glover's will reflects a measure of the testator's self-esteem and his sense of public duty as one of the principal men of the town. He requested the privilege of burial in

Corpus Christi choir in Grantham parish church and he ordered the distribution on that day of 20s in white bread among the poor of the town. At the conclusion of the will appears the hand of its author, 'by me John Wallis scripter'.[33]

John Wallis departed from his usual religious preamble when he wrote the will of the wealthy widow Anne Osland in 1597. As a godparent of one of his children, Anne Osland was linked by the tie of spiritual kinship to John Wallis, whom she affectionately called 'my gossypp' and whom she favoured with a gift of 3s 4d in her will, possibly in recognition of his services as well as his spiritual relationship. The lengthy and prolix preamble given in her will was clearly chosen in accordance with her personal religious susceptibilites rather than those of her scribe.

'I Anne Osland of Grantham (in the county of Lincoln) wyddowe ye unprofitable servant of god weake in body but strong in mynd . . . [do] willingly and with a free hart rendring and giving agayne into the hands of my lord god and creator my spirit wch he of his fatherly goodness gave unto me when he first fashioned mee in my mothers wombe making mee a living creature nothing dowting but that of his infinite mercyes set forth in the precious bloode of his dearly beloved sonne Jhesus Christ our alone Saviour and redeemer he will receave my soule into his glory and place y^t in the companye of heavenly Angells and blessed Sainctes . . .'[34]

Despite their apparent individuality, these words were not her own nor were they the composition of John Wallis. Identical phraseology had been employed on two previous occasions in Grantham wills, one as early as 1557.[35] Furthermore this particular preamble was known to Grantham willwriters and circulated within the community long before the publication of the same formula in 1590. In that year it appeared in a collection of precedents compiled by William West under the rather arcane title *Simboleography*.[36] The evidence would seem to suggest therefore that it was simply one of several accepted will formulae in circulation and not the composition of a local scribe. The case of Anne Osland's will cautions us against assuming a religious preamble, even an unusually extended one, to be the individual religious avowal of the willmaker, or moreover ascribing its composition to the originality of the scribe. Nevertheless the employment of an elaborate preamble like the one quoted above does suggest the intensity of the testator's religious convictions and the scribe's adoption of a suitable formula to accommodate those feelings.

TABLE 6

Occupational Structure of Grantham willmakers, 1501–1600.

Land:	gentry	5				Building		
	yeomen	23				carpenter	2	
	husbandmen	19				freemason	1	
		—					—	
		47	(33%)				3	(2%)
Industry:	Leather			Food &	baker		6	
	tanner	5		Drink:	butcher		4	
	glover	9			inkeeper		3	
	shoemaker	6					—	
	saddler	2					13	(9%)
		—		Services:	surgeon/barber		2	
		22	(15%)		servant		1	
	Cloth				miller		1	
	weaver	2					—	
	tailor	2					4	(3%)
	mercer	4		Clergy			2	(1%)
	woolmerchant	1		Misc.			4	(3%)
	woollendraper	2						
		—		*Status*:	political			
		11	(8%)		comburgesses		10	(7%)
	Metal				marital			
	blacksmith	3			widows		20	(14%)
	plumber	1			single women		2	(1%)
		—			bachelors		2	(1%)
		4	(3%)	Total			144	

When the ageing John Wallis came to write his own will in 1610, he was in poor health. Some seven years had elapsed since the last will he had written and during this period he had remarried, after losing his first wife and an adolescent son in the plague of 1604. In his final will, he committed his soul according to the familiar formula he had used in the past: 'I bequeath my soule into the handes of almighty god my maker of whome I trust to be saved by faith in Christ Jesus'.[37] John Wallis ordered a simple disposition of his goods. To his surviving eldest son he left, in addition to the best bed cover, 'my deske and all my bookes saveing three, that is,

Smyths sermons, the handfull of Hony Suckels, and the glasse of vaine glory', which three were reserved to his daughter Alice.[38] The residue of his goods was to be equally divided between his wife and daughter, with the wife enjoying the right of first choice. Although the will was written and read before witnesses, John Wallis neglected to nominate or sufficiently indicate his executor, and he was ironically deemed to have died intestate by the probate court. Letters of administration with the will annexed were issued to the widow who thereby undertook the responsibility of settling her late husband's estate.[39] In drafting wills therefore John Wallis generally employed a simple preamble of justification in conformity with official orthodoxy; where the testator insisted on a fuller exposition, John Wallis supplied the appropriate form.

Of the other scribes operating in Grantham less is known. The yeoman Thomas Patison wrote his own will in 1587 after several years experience as a frequent witness and occasional scribe at willmaking. Like John Wallis, he used a similar preamble in all the wills he wrote, including his own. His religious committal offered the testator's soul to god, 'trustinge that thorowe the merites of the passion of his dere sonne Jesus Christe he will receyve & accepte the same for righteous in his sight.'[40] In his own will Thomas Patison requested to be buried 'amongst my Bretherne and sisters against the Chernell howse windowe' and left four pence to old John the bellman to direct his executors to the place.[41] For the poor, he specified that 240 penny loaves be bought, cut in half and distributed on his burial day. Another scribe was Richard Smythe 'prieste vicare' of Grantham who wrote at least one will, although his presence as a witness in others similar in style and form suggests he was responsible for several more.[42] In 1559 the vicar was called upon to write and witness the will of the yeoman Thomas Kirkby, a service which was rewarded by his inclusion as a beneficiary, 'to vicare Smythe for writinge my will 3s 4d.'[43] Instituted a vicar in 1557, Richard Smythe appeared as a witness or scribe only for a short period of less than a year during his six year office. His hand is less apparent in the religious preambles than in the acts of piety contained in the wills he wrote or witnessed. Identical bequests in all five were made to the fabric of Lincoln cathedral and to the endowment of the high altar of the parish church, and nearly always to the poor of the town. Moreover, the vicar was often appointed a joint supervisor of the will. No comparable influence over testamentary gifts to the church or charity can be discerned in the wills written by other scribes.

Several scribes died without formulating their own wills. A later incumbent, Robert Bryan, vicar for fourteen years in the parish, wrote one will while he himself died intestate.[44] The yeoman Thomas Tompson appeared as a scribe in three wills and attested four others, but left no will.[45] All told, there were at least six scribes who died as intestates while only two concluded a will. Although willwriters were not professionals, there is some evidence of legal knowledge and godly education among them. John Hanson the butcher died intestate; but at one period of his life, he wrote three wills all affirming the testator's anticipation of election as co-heirs with Christ in eternity. Among his possessions were found 'one old Bible 1 old Statute booke & 3 other little bookes', evidence of his interest in religion and involvement in law.[46] Another scribe, William Busshey, from the marshland parish of Leverton, willed to his younger son, 'my Ieneva [sic] byble and a statute book', together with an assortment of implements for husbandry.[47]

In sum, the writers of wills in Grantham were not professional notaries. They were literate local yeomen, and to a lesser extent, parish clergymen, who possessed a basic legal understanding of willmaking; a knowledge acquired I would suggest as much from their practical experience as witnesses as from formal tuition in legal procedure. They were recognised in the community as willmakers and they could be relied upon to draft wills in legal form acceptable to the scrutiny of the church court. Their influence in will formulation was generally restricted to the required formulae and legalistic language in which the will was couched. Where the religious temper of the testator demanded a more explicit statement the scribe adopted a suitable formula to accommodate it; although the degree of latitude was in any event limited to formulae agreeable to church officials. An illustration of the strength of official orthodoxy is provided in the will of the Leverton widow Margaret Westland. Late in Edward's reign, she declared the supremacy of the king and bequeathed her soul 'to almighty god and to all the holly company in hevyn.' However, one of the officials of the probate court assiduously crossed out the reference to the saints in the register will, evidently in conformity with the doctrinal pronouncements of the Edwardian Reformation.[48] In general, therefore, it was left to the competence and discretion of the willwriter to provide an apposite religious preamble from a set of possible formulae. The practice of willwriting remained largely in the hands of non-professionals who performed this service on an irregular basis, being summoned at the request of the testator or his family.

Moving to broader conclusions then, wills are a valuable source revealing much about inheritance by will, the actual willmaking process itself, and family ties and attitudes within the willmaking community. But they must be used with caution and judgement. Any historical reconstruction of a local community based on wills must necessarily represent only a fraction of the community at large. It will be weighted towards the older, male and propertied sections of the community. Furthermore, a study founded on probate records is bound to heighten the apparent wealth of the community and to hide the poorer base of the community. Where personal attitudes are being examined, the circumstances of the will's formulation must be remembered – the physical weakness of the willmaker and the preparation for death. In addition, the influence of the scribe and the legal language employed must also be considered, particularly where the religious susceptibilities of the willmaker are under investigation. With the aid of parish registers, some of these problems can be partly resolved, as for example in determining the approximate size of the dying population or the burial dates of willmakers. Nevertheless the peculiarities of the source remain and these must be given due consideration in any historical research on probate records.

Notes

Abbreviations:

BL	British Library
FL	Foster Library
LAO	Lincolnshire Archives Office
LCC	Lincoln Consistory Court
PRO	Public Record Office
Resp	Responsa Personalia (Court Depositions)

1   M. Spufford, *Contrasting Communities. English villagers in the sixteenth and seventeenth centuries*, Cambridge, 1974.

2 A.J. Camp, *Wills and their whereabouts*, London, 4th edn, 1974, introd. p.ix.
3 R. Houlbrooke, *Church courts and the People during the English Reformation, 1520–1570,* Oxford, 1979, p.90.
4 John Sleford (12/12/1525). LAO.LCC Wills var./57.
5 Statute of Uses. 27 Hen. VIII, c.10. *Stat. Realm* III, pp. 539–42; Statute of Wills. 32 Hen. VIII, c.1 and Explanatory Act 34 Hen. VIII, c.5. *Stat. Realm* III, pp.744–6, 901–4.
6 Statute of Wills. 32 Hen. VIII, c.1.
7 H. Swinburne, *A briefe treatise of testaments and last wills* (1st publ. 1590–1), London, 1635 edn., pp.333 and 341.
8 Deposition of Thos. Blaunchard, labourer, Billinghay, Lincs. LAO. Resp. 3/f.68v. Will of Eliz Clerke, widow, Tattershall (9/3/1563/4). LAO. LCC Wills 1564/143.
9 Swinburne: 1635 edn., pp. 209–14.
10 Statute. 21 Hen. VIII, c.5. *Stat. Realm* III, pp.285–8.
11 BL Harleian Ms.618; printed in G.A.J. Hodgett, *Tudor Lincolnshire*. Lincoln, 1975, App.I, p.191.
12 For details on Grantham, see G.H. Martin, (ed.), *The Royal Charters of Grantham 1463–1688,* Leicester, 1963, introd., pp.9–18.
13 C.W. Foster (ed.), *Grantham Parish Register, 1562–1640,* Lincoln, 1916, p.149
14 John Aelmer, archdeacon of Lincoln and later bp. of London (1577–1594), was an exception in personally granting probate of wills in seven Grantham cases.
15 Houlbrooke, *op.cit.,* Table I, p.96. His figures for Norwich Consistory Court, Norfolk Archdeaconry Court and Surrey Archdeaconry Court are based on the period between date of willmaking and date of probate.
16 Robert Gregge (28/4/1588) bur. 4/5/1588. LAO. LCC Wills 1588/i/129
    Chris. Lupton (4/7/1594) bur.26/7/1594. LAO.LCC Wills 1544/ii/181
    Ric. Primette (6/2/1584) bur. 12/2/1583/4. LAO.LCC Wills 1583/i/147.
17 For the jurisdiction of the PCC in the diocese of Lincoln, see M. Bowker, 'The supremacy and the episcopate: the struggle for control, 1534–40', *Historical Journal* 18 (1975), 240–1.
18 Wm. Smythe (11/4/1582). bur. 14/4/1582 prob. 19/4/1582. PRO PCC Prob. 11/64/91.
19 R.A. Marchant, *The Church under the law: Justice, administration and discipline in the diocese of York, 1560–1640,* Cambridge, 1969, p.88.
20 From unpublished findings kindly given to me by Sarah Harrison, research assistant to Alan Macfarlane, Social Anthopology Dept., Cambridge. (7 Feb. 1979).
21 Wm. Bland (26/6/1599). LAO. LCC Wills 1600/166. Inv. 93/389. Thos. Russell (17/5/1595). LAO.LCC Wills 1595/ii/48–51. Inv. 86/305.
22 Gloria Main, 'Probate records as a source for early American history', *William and Mary Quarterly,* 32 (1975), p.96.
23 Harry Scot (13/3/1569/70). LAO.LCC Wills 1570/195.
    Robert Gregge (28/4/1588). bur. 4/5/1588. LAO.LCC Wills 1588/i/129.
24 P. Aries, *Western attitudes toward death,* Baltimore, 1974, pp. 7–11 and 40–1.
25 Matthew Peyke (29/12/1557). LAO.LCC Wills 1558/ii/55v–56v.
26 Jo. Richardson (1557). LAO.LCC 1557/iii/161.

27 Deposition of Thos. East, vicar of Owersby, Lincs. LAO. Resp. 3/128. Will of
    Jane Clerk, 'vergyn', Owersby (31/5/1566).
28 A pioneering study of wills and their scribes is found in M. Spufford, 'The
    scribes of villagers' wills in the sixteenth and seventeenth century Cam-
    bridgeshire and their influence', *Local Population Studies*, 7(1971), 28–43. Her
    work has prompted the search by others for the existence of will precedent
    books from which the scribe may have taken the religious preamble and other
    legal phraseology. See *LPS* 8 (1972), 55–7; 9 (1972), 33–42; 14 (1975), 49–50;
    17 (1976), 42–3; and 19 (1977), 35–6.
29 Deposition in the form of a letter by Wm. Harrison, vicar of Kirton in
    Holland, to Thos. Tailour, registrar of the Archdeaconry of Lincoln, Oct.
    1567. LAO. Resp. 3/130. Will of Marion Alben, widow, Kirton in Holland.
    LAO.LCC Wills 1567/189v.–190.
30 Jas. Wallis, merchant of the Staple (27/4/1577). Died over 11 years later.
    LAO.LCC Wills 1588/ii/42.
31 Robert Wallis wrote the wills of Jo. Wollands, bachelor (31/12/1591) and
    Isabel Bringam, singlewoman (2/8/1592). LAO.LCC Wills 1591 i/463; 1592/2
    No adm. is recorded for Robert Wallis, bur. 13/9/1595.
32 Leonard Gyfforth, glover (6/4/1599). LAO.LCC Wills 1599/94v–96
    Jo. Laborne, saddler (5/10/1603). LCC Wills 1604/ii/120
    Ralph Locco, comburgess (9/10/1597). LCC Wills 1597/256
    Jo. Brotherton, comburgess (12/3/1587/8). LCC Wills 1590/104.
33 Jo. Brotherton (12/3/1587/8). LAO.LCC Wills 1590/104.
34 Anne Osland, widow (16/7/1597) LAO.LCC Wills 1600/22–23v.
35 Simon Clarkson, vicar of Grantham (12/7/1557). LAO.LCC Wills 1558/ii/8
    Simon Hanson, comburgess (20/2/1575/6). LCC Wills 1576/16.
36 William West, *Simboleography* (1st edn. 1590) Pt.1, section 642.
    Eric Poole, who first drew attention to the printed will precedent, argues
    that the wills cited by M. Spufford as bearing religious preambles of a highly
    individual expression resemble very much in fact the form given in the
    precedent book. See Eric Poole, 'Will formularies', *Local Population Studies*,
    17 (1976), 42–3. cf. M. Spufford, *Contrasting Communities*, pp. 341–2 and her
    reply in *LPS* 19 (1977), 35–6.
37 Jo. Wallis (16/8/1610). LAO.LCC Wills 1610/64.
38 *Ibid.*
39 Jo. Wallis. LAO.LCC adm.B./84.
40 Thos. Symson, glover (13/11/1586). LAO.LCC Wills 1586/279–80.
41 Thos. Patison (19/1/1586/7). LAO.LCC Wills 1587/430–1.
42 Ric. Smythe, vicar of North Grantham, 1557–1563, compounded with South
    Grantham 24/4/1560. LAO. FL e.7.
43 Thos. Kirkby (20/1/1558/9). LAO.LCC Wills 1558/i/156.
44 Robert Bryan, vicar of South Grantham, 1586–1600, compounded with North
    Grantham 4/11/1586–1596. LAO.FL e.7. Adm. BI 1600/11. Wrote the will of
    Edw. Orson, weaver (28/8/1588). LAO.LCC 1588/ii/53.
45 Thos. Tompson. LAO.1570 Adm. Act Bk ii/76. Wrote the wills of Robert
    Taylor (22/7/1556). LAO.LCC Wills 1556–7/129; Simon Bower, servant
    (12/1/1556/7). LCC Wills 1553–6/178; Thos. Tilson, butcher and comburgess
    (10/5/1570). LCC Wills.

46　Jo. Hanson (9/5/1622) LAO.LCC Adm.I. 1622/27.
47　Wm. Busshey (26/7/1588) husbandman, Leverton, Lincs. LAO.LCC Wills
　　1588/ii/155–7.
48　Margaret Westland (4/3/1552/3) widow, Leverton. LAO.LCC Wills 1552–
　　6/226.

PROBATE INVENTORIES AND PROVINCIAL RETAILERS IN THE SEVENTEENTH CENTURY

D.G. Vaisey

My purpose in this paper is twofold.* To make some general comments about probate inventories from a somewhat different point of view to that of most of you and then to bring out some of the points which my perusal of retailers' inventories over the years has caused me to consider. I am, as you have gathered, first and foremost a custodian of records rather than a researcher. It is, of course, a poor custodian who is not also a researcher; but I am a keeper by instinct and not a plunderer. I feel rather as did the late Harry Bell, the historian of the Court of Wards, who reminisced in a lecture to undergraduates about his younger days in the 1930's when he switched roles from being a research student to being an assistant keeper in the Public Record Office:

'In Cambridge', he said, 'I had been interested in the gathering, arrangement, and interpretation of historical facts; but the

---

* In the five years which have elapsed between the delivery of this paper and its publication the study of probate inventories has greatly advanced. This advance has not altered to any significant degree the views which I expressed in 1979, but three points need to be made in the light of recent developments. Margaret Spufford's work mentioned on p. 107 has now been published as *The Great Reclothing of Rural England: Petty Chapmen and their Wares in the Seventeenth Century* (1984); Clare Gitting's findings referred to in footnote 17 have been incorporated in her *Death, Burial and the Individual in Early Modern England* (1984); and the probate documents cited as being in the Bodleian Library were transferred in 1984 to the Berkshire and Oxfordshire Record Offices. Though their location has changed their numerical references remain unaltered.

processes whereby such facts are originally established had been outside my ken. My first experience of the Records was, therefore, something of a shock, both as to their bulk and the difficulties of interpretation that seemed to surround them. Professor Galbraith has described how, under similar circumstances, he found it more difficult to accept, or take seriously, the facile generalisations of the great literary historians. This is really what happened to me. I became increasingly preoccupied with the significance of the original source; I grew into a document snob, and I have been one ever since.'[1]

Harry Bell was not a snob of course, and could never have been accused of developing the local historian's documentary 'tunnel vision' at which it is fashionable now to scoff. But as a manuscript librarian or an archivist I must act, as he did then, as a servicing agent to the historical industry. If there are plumbers and plumbers' mates, there are also historians and historians' mates. I am a historians' mate and as such part of my role is to provide historians with the most relevant and apt tools for their job. But a craftsman's mate often develops an interest in one side of the work rather than another. Further, often merely by handling the tools more frequently than any individual master, he gets to reflecting on the quality of the tools, and whether his master is making the best use of them. One of my own continuing special areas of interest is that of the nature of provincial shops in the seventeenth century, and for some years I have been collecting and noting down information upon them in whatever geographical area I happen to have been; and I happen now to be in Oxford. My research – if research it can be called – has been directed to no particular end, nor has it been hammered into shape to bolster any particular thesis. Not much of it has yet been followed through exhaustively to any conclusion, but if my notes are angled in any direction they are angled from the point of view of the consumer. I have set myself the limited task of providing answers to such questions as: what, from the point of view of the man in the street in Oxford in the seventeenth century, did a mercer's shop contain? Or a haberdasher's? But, as always, in finding materials to answer these basic questions, one finds oneself questioning more general statements. Is it true, as Dorothy Davis said in her *History of Shopping,* that 'Only rarely can we get a glimpse of retail trade in this century from the point of view of the shopkeeper'?[2] Again, some economic historians seem to base the contention that there were few retailers or providers of transport services in seventeenth-century England not on hard facts but on the theory that there was no need for them. Is that true? Is it true, as is always said by historians of the book trade, that because of the presence there of presses and the universities, only in Oxford and Cambridge (outside London) could booksellers survive unaided by finance from some other trade?

I could not hope to answer all these questions in the space of a short paper even if I *knew* the answers, but on this latter question my own work seems to indicate that it is not true. Most booksellers in Oxford needed to diversify into more lucrative businesses, and unless they got a foothold themselves or obtained loans from others with a stake in the lucrative business of food and drink, they were likely to go to the wall. But that is really the subject of another paper. I will return to it briefly later on, but I will limit myself here to saying that there is an illuminating thesis to be written on the role in seventeenth-century Oxford of the college manciples: men heavily involved in the food and drink business, tied up with the university but running shops, inns and other establishments on their own account, and acting as entrepreneurs in many other trades.

To return to my simple questions: customers' account books give a sight of goods after they have been bought, and in Oxford a document as meticulous as the diary of Anthony Wood provides a detailed picture of the shopping habits of a sober-sided don.[3] But one class of document which often does give us a view from inside the shop is, of course, the probate inventory and its related documents. Thus along with my interest in shops has gone an interest in this particular key for opening them. They are, as John Moore pointed out, a common and plentiful enough source, but I will, if I may, make a few comments on their use which I think should be made. The first is this: that too often they are used, or at least made available, at their face value without taking into account evidence provided by the documents which go with them in the matter of probate. And the second is that the accepted way of making probate inventories available in print has been to take a geographical area – a county, a parish, or a town, and to publish the available probate inventories for that area between given dates. We all know, and have used, the standard collections: from those early Surtees Society volumes through to John Moore's Frampton Cot-

terell series[4] and the Chesterfield ones of J.M. Bestall's class.[5] Along
the way Francis Steer, Michael Havinden, Peter Kennedy, Margaret
Cash, myself and others have gone on producing these topographi-
cally-based volumes – usually through the local Record Society.
Now, local Record Society volumes are not in general noted for the
excellence of their subject indexes, and so anyone interested in a
topic other than agriculture is condemned to conducting a large
trawling operation through the volumes in order to find the information of value to him. And when a particularly interesting specialist
inventory is discovered and made the subject of a set-piece article in
a specialist journal, it tends to give the impression that such things
are a good deal more unusual than in fact they are, and than the
author may think. I have myself fallen into this trap with the
inventories of shopkeepers, and it is almost certainly true I should
say of, for instance, Francis Steer's 'The Possessions of a Sussex
Surgeon'[6] which used as its text the will and probate inventory of
William Whighte, surgeon, of Midhurst, who died early in 1632.

It seems to me that the time has now come for more specialized
volumes, so that we can avoid falling into the trap already sprung by
editors of another kind of social document in which I have developed an interest: the Victorian photograph. The immediate
appeal of these documents is such that volume after volume is
produced, with little critical editing, simply because they are there.
Probate inventories share with the Victorian photograph the virtues
of being plentiful and having an immediate lay appeal, but the
virtues do not always lead to their sensible exploitation. We can also
avoid that other trap to which I have referred – that of treating as
abnormal what would be the norm if we only took the trouble to find
enough examples. We need now to have volumes of blacksmiths'
inventories over a wide area, of booksellers' inventories, inventories
of mercers and apothecaries and surgeons so that we do not have to
erect hypotheses of professions upon random published examples as
has, for instance, T.S. Willan in his book of essays about provincial
shopkeepers in the sixteenth and seventeenth centuries.[7]

Having said that, and having alluded to medical men, let us look
briefly at the probate papers of town apothecaries and surgeons.
The first man I want to mention was not an Oxford apothecary but
an Abingdon one. His name was John Mayott and he died in
October 1686. His will, which he had made early in the previous
month was taken for probate to the Berkshire archdeacon's court

and remains amongst the probate papers of that court in the Bodleian Library.[8] One interesting point is that he styled himself 'gentleman' in his will: it was his neighbours who called him 'apothecary' when they drew up the inventory – a revealing difference of viewpoint when it comes to considering status. To his brother Richard he left 'my Plaster Box with the Instruments therein and my Salvatory and my Case of Lancetts with the Instruments therein', and Richard was also bequeathed 'Soe many of my Books relateing to Phisick or Chirurgier as he shall thinke fitt to Choose whether they be wrote in Greeke, Lattin or English', together with the two cases they were in. His wife was to have the rest of his books. All his drugs, medicines, medicaments, pots, glasses, boxes, shelves, drawers, counters, mortars (except the middle-sized one), presses, plaster pans, furnaces, and stills, together with the shop books and the debts in them 'and alsoe all other untencills and things which I have belonging to the Art of a Chirurgion or Apothecary' were also to go to Richard provided that he was not out of his apprenticeship. But if he was out of his apprenticeship, 'sett upp for himself and trading in the Art of an Apothecary or Chirurgion', then they were to go to the widow.

The inventory shows that Mayott's house apparently consisted of kitchen, buttery, and shop on the ground floor; chambers over the kitchen and shop on the first floor; and a garret over each on the second floor. The absence of any kind of main living room or hall is a little baffling though we do seem to have a complete house here. The Mayotts seem to have been a childless couple whose main living quarters were upstairs. The goods in the shop and house, together with debts due to the deceased, were valued at £387 17s 5d. The books which he had left to his brother were in the garret over the kitchen and were valued at £2 10s, although they were not, alas, listed by title. Also in that room were the case of lancets with a razor and incision knife valued at 10s and the plaster box with instruments valued at 15s. They, too, went to Richard, as did the entire contents of the shop. These contents appraised by another apothecary and a milliner are itemized in some detail and, in all, come to £46 12s 11d. It is interesting to contrast this sum with that given for the debts due to him which amounted to some £290–£150 of which was classed as desperate and to be written off. If therefore this inventory is a true reflection of Mayott's wealth, it shows that three-quarters of it was tied up in debts owing to him which were, of course, likely to have

been investments; and of the remaining quarter almost 50% represented stock in the shop.

From the dry details of what was there we can get the feel of a
later seventeenth-century apothecary's shop. There was the counter
with, behind it, a nest of drawers containing drugs and, in front of it,
a similar nest of boxes; there were in the shop at least three other
nests of small drawers containing drugs, 141 more small boxes
arranged in four nests, and, in addition, a great wainscot box and a
large tub containing drugs in parcels. On the counter stood two
drawers in a stand (a primitive till, perhaps), a pair of scales and
weights, pewter measures and three mortars and pestles. There
were fourteen herb barrels, together with galley pots, pill pots,
electuary, conserve and ointment pots, oil pots and syrup pots,
running in number to at least 175; and at least fourteen dozen glass
jars or bottles of various sizes and for various purposes. Thirty-eight
more of his books were kept in a closet in the shop.

Details of the stock are none too precise. The appraisers were
perhaps too pressed for time or considered it unnecessary to go into
great detail. There are headings for 'chymicall oyls'; 'powders
simple and compound'; simple, distilled and compound waters;
'syrups'; 'tinctures and spirits of divers kinds'; and similar portman-
teau entries. There is mention of mithridate and diascordium, spirits
of wine, and spirits of hartshorn, which most laymen would have
recognised, but there is nothing like the information on stock such
as is to be found in the inventory of the Lichfield apothecary,
Samuel Newboult, in 1666, and which was included in my Lichfield
collection.[9] To a non-chemist such as myself some of the named
drugs in Newboult's shop verge on the comic: sanguis dragonis,
pomegranate pills, virgin's wax, black soap – but Culpeper shows
that they had their uses and they all had their origins. In this
apothecary's house in the centre of England were drugs and specifics
originating from China, the East Indies, Northern India, North
America, Mexico, the West Indies, Asia Minor, Spain, Ceylon,
North Africa and all parts of Europe. And besides his drugs he also
sold sweetmeats: macaroons, caraway comfits, candied fruits and
brown sugars, as well as soap, salt, vinegar and tobacco. In the
previous year the apothecary's shop of the widow Katherine Seall of
Birmingham, for whom there is a detailed probate inventory,[10] was
over a cellar containing a variety of commodities, including honey,
figs, raisins, molasses and soap.

The probate package is a good source for showing us what was meant when the seventeenth century gave a trade or status name to a man. Already we have seen a man who called himself 'gentleman' being seen as an apothecary by his neighbours and having a shop which bears that out. Similarly, one of only two shopkeepers whom I have found specialising in pottery in seventeenth-century Abingdon was known as a yeoman.[11] Too many studies in the social and economic history of the seventeenth century and, in particular studies of towns, still seem to me to make too much of the distinction between gentlemen, yeomen, and tradesmen or professionals. Numbers of gentlemen and yeomen are totted up and equated with 'the landed interest' in a way which these documents show is unwise. In towns, documents such as these inventories do illustrate well how status names meant different things to different people, and how they came and went with the generations.

They also show us the range of quality, as it were, within any one status category. The apothecaries Samuel Newboult of Lichfield and John Mayott of Abingdon, and the apothecary's widow Katherine Seall of Birmingham, with their well-to-do establishments and their large quantity of stock diversified into various lines, make a good contrast with the apothecary Nicholas Cooke of Barnstaple whose inventory was drawn up in February 1694/5.[12] He was worth a little over £81 but the stock in his shop was valued at a mere £15 – only £3 10s more than the valuation put upon his clothes – and the general impression gained from this document is of a more narrowly-based practitioner. Interestingly, his is the only such inventory I have seen which mentions and values the 'Coate of Armes that belongs to an Apothecary': this might have been his shop sign, as undoubtedly was the 'Naked Boy' which Samuel Newboult had in the window of his Lichfield establishment. But otherwise there is an air of oddness about the Barnstaple list. He had, for instance, at least 31 leather chairs and four dozen of old and much worn plates, six feather beds of which four were called bad and the other two indifferent good, nine old rugs of which five were termed 'very bad', a part of a screen, and the only cooking kettle he had was described as old and full of holes. Although he possessed some of the trappings of the civilized man such as pictures, maps, books, wine glasses and a 'scriptorey' or writing case, all was evidently not well with the apothecary of Barnstaple. However, we need more examples before we decide whether he or his Midland colleagues represented the norm.

The usefulness of probate inventories for pointing up what was meant by a trade or professional designation, and the range of practitioners within it, is demonstrated again in the case of provincial surgeons. Edward Stevens was a surgeon in Henley-on-Thames who died in 1663.[13] His will, made some two months before his death, shows that he had three sons under 21, a wife – Clara – and a brother in Leigh-on-Sea in Essex, who was also a surgeon. The eldest son, Thomas, was to have his father's 'Box of silver Instruments' but no other tools or marks of his profession are mentioned. The inventory shows the house to have been on three floors with four chambers at first floor level or above. At ground floor level there was a hall, kitchen, washhouse, shop, warehouse and cellar. If it seems strange for a surgeon to have had a shop, the contents of it and of the warehouse may seem even stranger. The shop contained £110-worth of 'apothecary surrups and drugs and haberdaishers wares and grossery', while the warehouse had in it no less than £83.10s. worth of salt, vinegar, sugar and currants, £19 10s worth of raisins, prunes, tobacco, paper, white starch, spices, alum and dye, and £20 10s worth of soap, strong waters, treacle, empty gallipots, glasses and fuel for firing. His study of books (alas unnamed) and instruments for surgery were valued at a mere £10 out of a total of some £365.

If these documents show, then, that the term 'yeoman' (which some continue to equate with the landed interest) embraced tradesmen who dealt primarily in pottery, and that the term 'gentleman' included apothecaries, they also show that the term 'surgeon' could cover a man two-thirds of whose wealth was tied up in haberdashery and grocery. These trade and professional inventories therefore point up the difference which can exist between what a man was called and what he apparently was. But, of course, in saying that, we are delivering ourselves into the hands of the appraisers. Can a list of goods, drawn up often by friends of the family rather than by impartial appraisers, against which a deceased person's debts could be set, convey a true picture of the house, goods, farm implements, trading stock, or whatever which the deceased possessed during his life? I have come to have rather more doubts about it than did John Moore in his paper. There is often a distinction between what a man owned and what he enjoyed; and the clues to this distinction are often provided not by the inventory but by the other probate papers – the will, or (in the case of intestacy) the administration bond, and (also in the case of intestacy) the administrator's accounts.

I will illustrate this point with an example from Lichfield.[14] On 9 July 1673 three appraisers listed the goods, room by room, of William Thorneworke, a paviour, who died without leaving a will; and on 1 August administration of her deceased husband's effects was granted to the widow, Anne Thorneworke. Here, it might be thought (since this is obviously a complete house), is a picture of William and Anne Thorneworke's house and its contents. But in the administration papers Anne is called Anne Thorneworke *alias* Reade. Now also on 9 July the same three appraisers listed the goods, room by room, of a Richard Reade; and on 1 August again administration of Reade's estate was granted to Anne Reade, his widow. A comparison of the two inventories reveals that the same house was being visited in both, although the goods are quite different and some items, deleted from one inventory, appear in the other. The conclusion to be drawn must be that when Anne's second husband died she withheld her first husband's goods from the appraisers as not being liable for his debts, and took the opportunity, while the appraisers were there and while she was about probate business, to take out administration papers for her first husband's goods. This is important, for the two inventories together produce a completely different picture from that given by either one on its own. This is particularly so in the matter of room usage. The parlour, for example – a room at this time in transition from a sleeping room to a sitting room – appears as a poorly furnished sitting room in Thorneworke's inventory, and in Reade's as a room with a bed in it. Taken together, the two inventories show it to have been a relatively well-furnished sitting and sleeping room of the standard type.

The point I am making here is that even a document which inventories a complete house with what could well be its complete furnishings, may, in fact, have left out another almost equally complete set of goods which, had they been included, would give us the true picture of the style in which the deceased person lived.

In other cases I could quote, an analysis of the bequests given in a will can show a person who appears from an inventory to have been in humble, if not straightened, circumstances, to have had assets in goods, money and property far in excess of that given in the inventory: and again, others in which whole rooms in the house are mentioned whose existence is not obvious from the inventory; and yet more where the will mentions working arrangements for a tradesman who, from the inventory, appears to have ceased work. For example, the will of one Thomas Smythe,[15] a gunsmith of Thame, drawn up in July 1643, made specific bequests to his three children. The eldest son, Thomas, was to have the goods in his parlour, the chamber over it, and the cockloft over that; his second son, Richard, the goods and tools in the shop, the chamber over it, and the cockloft over that; and his daughter, Susanna, the goods in the cellar and the hall, the chamber over it, and the cockloft over that. No kitchen is mentioned, and the widow was to have the use of it all during her life. He was dead by 1 May 1644 when the inventory was drawn up, and probate was granted to the widow in July. The contents of neither shop nor hall appear in the inventory, though a kitchen is mentioned. One of the cocklofts at least seems to have been empty. Several interpretations could be put on this discrepancy, of course. But the important thing is that there is a discrepancy: many of the volumes of published inventories (most of them edited by archivists, I am sorry to say) would not have picked it up.

A matter, too, which is often overlooked is that in interpreting an inventory it is important to know to whom probate or administration was being granted. Cases where a will of an apparently wealthy man is followed by the inventory of an apparently poor man are often explained by following probate through to discover that the appointed executors refused to serve, and that administration was then granted to the principal creditor.

Lastly, it is generally and of necessity, assumed that many estates over which there was no contention were never submitted for probate in order to save expense. We have seen that this must have happened in the case of Anne Thorneworke's first husband. It seems to me an equally valid assumption that in other non-contentious cases which did go to probate there was no need to be over-zealous in the drawing up of an inventory. The point that I am making here, rather laboriously I am afraid, is that to use inventories and especially to publish them without scrutinizing their accompanying papers is folly, and that this is all too often done.

Granted then that they have flaws which are not obvious – so to say – with the naked eye, it follows that any argument from silence based on probate inventories is extremely dangerous. The case I always quote is that though I have seen hundreds of probate inventories listing flocks of sheep, I have never seen one that lists a dog. One would not, therefore, dream of saying that no sheepdogs were used in the seventeenth century. One knows that this is not true. Yet in areas of greater dispute (and perhaps greater moment) such as the evidence for the ownership of books in the seventeenth century, one has heard and seen statements based on inventory evidence that whereas most households in such and such an area possessed a Bible, only a small percentage possessed anything else. Such statements seem to me to misunderstand the attitude and role of the appraisers: while most might be relied upon to recognise a Bible, they are likely to have had neither the time, the inclination, nor the education to note down any others unless they were especially grand or were present in large enough numbers to be valued as goods in their own right – and then one has occasionally come across specialists being brought in to value them, since they were regarded as peculiar items. Otherwise the convenient phrase 'other lumber' would cover them, or they would be considered unworthy of the valuers' notice lying in a chest, cupboard or chest of drawers, along with the other little bits of bric-a-brac which houses must have contained but which one doesn't find in the inventories. Further, even this leaves out of account the widow, child, or other interested party who doubtless kept his eye on the appraisers, saying of any item: 'Don't put that in, it wasn't his.' Here I disagree in some measure with John Moore. I think there was often as strong a pressure on appraisers to get things wrong as to get things right.

Those who know Ben Jonson's play *Volpone* will recall that at one point Volpone pretends to be dead in order to trick his neighbours and hangers-on.[16] When these people come to call he instructs his servant Mosca to act as if his master had just died: 'Get thee a cap', he says, 'a counte booke, pen and inke, papers before thee; sit, as thou wert taking an inventory of parcels'. When the visitors, who expect to benefit from Volpone's death, see Mosca being so assiduous, they applaud his thoroughness. 'I like his care', one of them says. But when they discover that Mosca is the heir and that they are excluded, they are quick to point out that such and such an item had been given to them in Volpone's lifetime and should not be in the inventory. Inventories, then, can be good evidence of things being in a particular place, but are of little use as evidence of things *not* being in a particular place.

One further point about probate papers which I must mention, and that is that the administrator's account, where it survives, has been very little used by social and economic historians. This is, as you know, the list of charges which, in cases of intestacy or where the executorship of a will was declined, the administrator put into the court to be set off against the inventory total. Quite apart from anything else, these documents are a marvellous source for evidence not of the cost of living, but of the cost of dying in the seventeenth century. A recently submitted M. Litt. thesis at Oxford by Clare Gittings showed their usefulness in this respect.[17] But they have many other uses. Debts owed *to* the deceased should appear in the inventory, but these accounts, particularly in the case of tradesmen, in setting out the debts owed *by* the estate, can show where that person was obtaining his financial backing. And, balanced against the inventory, they can give a more accurate picture of the tradesman's standing.

Let us look at the case of John Badcock, a privileged person of the university in Oxford. That is to say, he was a tradesman but one who as a servant of the university, was licenced to trade not by a city company but by the university. As such he was matriculated and could claim the privileges of a member of the university, including the right to be heard in the university court. He was a carrier, and he died early in 1708 without leaving a will. Administration was granted to the widow, and an inventory of his premises in Holywell, which he rented from Merton College, was drawn up.[18] On the evidence of this inventory he died a wealthy man – the sum total was £923 6s 10d.

The inventory appears on its own evidence to give an incomplete picture of this three-storey house: it mentions a room over the shop but no shop or its contents are listed nor does there seem to be a proper kitchen. This may be evidence that he was in partnership, and that the goods in the shop were not his. However, this large total included the value of his lease (£113), trading debts owing to him of £555 7s, stock in the way of timber, firewood and coal of £80 16s, and twelve horses valued at £45 10s, but (strangely) no waggons. The horses, interestingly, are listed by name, and include such traditional names for heavy draught animals as Scott, Wagg, Whitefoot, Duke, Punch, Darby, Robin and Sorrell.

In April 1709 the estate was wound up when the widow put in her account to the court.[19] Badcock had evidently had a fairly lavish funeral (oysters were even accounted for) and several large bills had had to be paid, including one for hops of £41 and another to the glazier of £70. A large number of the debts owed to the deceased had had to be written off as desperate: these were mainly from college men who had gone abroad, died, couldn't be found, or who had vanished into the fastnesses of Wales, Barbados, and similar parts. When all had been totted up the estate was left with £116 17s 3d – just £38 19s 1d for each of the three beneficiaries: a very different picture from that gained from the inventory alone.

To take another example from many. In June 1633 Thomas Clarke, another priviliged person in Oxford, made his will.[20] He was a cook, and cooks were often very well-to-do persons, making a good living from colleges, taverns and inns. The will made many bequests to his relatives and friends and he left a ring to the President of St John's College whom he wished to be his executor. But the inventory, when it was drawn up in October of 1633, listed goods to the value of £11 12s 8d only. If we look at the court act books we find that on 19 July the President of St John's returned the ring and refused the executorship; and a month later on 19 August the widow also declined to serve in that capacity. Administration was thus granted to Christopher Horne, yeoman, and John Blunt, a city mercer, who were two of the deceased's creditors, and it was they who put the inventory into court. The inventory itself looks seriously undervalued: 33 lb of brass for instance were valued at only 11s. Two years later, in July 1635, Horne put in the account to wind up the estate. It is clear from this account that Blunt had been paid off from the goods and from a lump sum claimed from the Company of Cooks of Oxford by way of death benefit, but the estate was not big enough for Horne to recover all of his smaller debt, and he had been further put to the expense of £2 in court actions staving off other creditors claiming sums amounting to over £80. Again, to use that probate inventory or the will in isolation as evidence of Clarke's standing in the community would be seriously to mistreat the documents.

Having, then, made these general points about the use of probate inventories as evidence, I want now to take them purely as evidence of what was listed by the appraisers, and to get back to my original limited aim of seeing what goods were stocked by what tradesmen in the Oxford area in the seventeenth century. The additional point probably needs to be made that we cannot expect a shopkeeper's holdings of fresh food to be reflected in these documents, since, being liable to rapid decay, much of it would in a short time be valueless in the appraisers' eyes. An interesting example of this occurs in the inventory of Nicholas Oram, an Oxford fishmonger, made in January 1688/9.[21] His shop contained whiting, rabbits, neats' tongues, sturgeon, lobsters and oysters – all things which the January cold would preserve – but the oranges and lemons were put down as frost-bitten. Oram, incidentally (and this is quite irrelevant to this paper), also possessed an item which I have seen in no other inventory – 'A little howse for children to play with'.

The wealthy general dealers in the Oxford area were the mercers. By the seventeenth century the term 'mercer' was in many areas virtually interchangeable with that of 'grocer'. This latter designation seems not to have been much used in Oxford where, if the term 'mercer' was interchangeable with any, it was with 'chandler', though it was never completely so. Both mercers and chandlers were general dealers in all kinds of hardware and foods but each was firmly based on its own specialities. I have come across, for instance, only one shopkeeper calling himself 'potter' in this area: this was George Ecton of Abingdon who died in 1696 and whose probate inventory is in print.[22] But some mercers evidently made a speciality of stocking and selling ceramics, stoneware and glass. A large proportion of the goods in the shop of Robert Ellis of Oxford, for instance, a mercer who died in 1597, was represented by this kind of commodity, and in addition he had a 'workinge chamber' which, from the nature of the goods in it, seems to indicate that he was actively engaged in the making, or at least the decoration, of stoneware and pottery.[23]

Similarly, the establishment of James Pen, known as a chandler but called 'grocer' by Anthony Wood and who was manciple of St John's College, contained enormous numbers of glasses and bottles.[24] It seems likely that he sold drink for consumption on or off the premises, though in fact the inventory, made in 1642, listed only vinegar in barrels, apart, that is, from barrels of rice, anchovies, currants, raisins and salt. The administrator's accounts show that he had large debts to beerbrewers though these may have been incurred in his business of provisioning St John's College. But the picture given by the inventory is of a wealthy candle-maker of the normal type, with a definite speciality in the drink side of the business. Artificial light was expensive in the seventeenth century, but I suspect, as I have said before, that there was more profit for the shopkeeper in drink. Pen, in fact, had a detached workhouse on a separate lease in which his candle manufacturing was carried on, though other chandlers appear to have rendered down their tallow and dipped and moulded their candles in the cellars beneath their shops, which must have made the streets of Oxford fairly unsavoury at times of manufacture. Pen's premises *had* a large cellar which is still to be seen, but he used it for the storage of large quantities of dry goods, vinegar and earthenware. It is interesting to note again in passing that the only other shopkeeper I have come upon in this area apparently specializing in earthenware and ceramics is John Bartlett of Abingdon in 1675 who was styled neither 'mercer', 'chandler' nor 'potter', but 'yeoman', though neither his will nor his inventory betrays any connection with agriculture.[25]

Mercers were the least specialized of all shopkeepers and, on the evidence afforded by my work, it would seem that most small towns and large villages would have sported a mercer's shop, even if there were no others save perhaps a blacksmith, and even if on market days they were served by chapmen financed and furnished with goods by the bigger tradesmen from Oxford or a nearby large town. But in these larger towns the probate inventories of mercers, where the appraisers were both knowledgeable and assiduous, show what emporia some of their establishments were. If we take as an example the stock of William Clarke of the parish of All Saints in Oxford, who died in 1612, we can see this well.[26] His stock contained, as might be expected, many kinds of cloth ranging from sackcloth to lawn, from canvas to holland, from serge to taffeta and from linsey woolsey and fustian to cambric and silk. And he possessed these cloths in many different qualities, widths and colours. Besides this cloth in the piece, he sold all kinds of threads, buttons, points, laces, ribbons and silks to decorate garments once made. But the appraisers listed few made-up items from cloth and wool, save for table-napkins, hose and stockings, girdles and garters. Clarke stocked the latter in many different grades, the most expensive valued at 4s a pair: these were perhaps the most eye-catching, for garters were designed to be seen and not hidden. The virtual absence of ready-made clothing from this early seventeenth-century shop is interesting. When Anthony Wood wrote of buying a suit or a coat from his mercer, he meant buying the length of cloth for such a garment. He subsequently went to his tailor to have it made up, and tailors' inventories show them to have been poor tradesmen owning little save for their working tools, and making up clothes to the customer's specification from cloth bought by the customer not from them, but from the mercers.

That there was a demand for ready-made clothing, especially for children, is evidenced by the arrival in Oxford during the century of shopkeepers calling themselves milliners, who attempted to fill this need. Milliners at this date were not the hat and bonnet makers they were to become: that field in seventeenth-century Oxford was reserved to the haberdashers and cappers. The milliners' arrival led to a series of legal and commercial battles about which papers survive in both university and city archives: battles between them and the tailors. But by the end of the century the milliners were firmly entrenched; and by the 1670's we have good evidence from probate inventories of milliners' shops well stocked with gowns and mantles, coats, skirts, trousers, drawers, frocks, petticoats, bodices, cloaks and children's wear.

Clarke, the 1612 mercer, however, stocked many other commodities besides cloth. On the hardware side there were nails and screws, spurs, bits, stirrups and other horse furniture, chains, pouches, candlesticks, snuffers and links, padlocks, whipcord and bowstrings, combs and brushes, purses and pincushions, paper and ink, pitch, starch, soaps, whitewash, gunpowder and shot. He stocked items as varied as sucking bottles for babies, sets of chessmen, tobacco, hops, and basic books such as grammars, primers and ABC's, as well as hornbooks. On what we should now think of as the grocery side, his goods were also varied: here one could have bought raisins and currants, treacle and sugar, honey, almonds and comfits, dates and prunes, and spices such as cinnamon, cumin seed, ginger, nutmeg, pepper, mustard seed, aniseed, onion seed, bay berries, fenugreek, mace, saffron, capers, olives and cloves. Magdalen College alone owed him £22 for spices. Other mercers' stock contains in addition apothecary's wares in the way of primitive medicines, but only two commodities of this kind appear in Clarke's inventory: wormseed to purge the intestines of parasites and stavesacre against the lice.

The inventories of Oxford mercers, too, seem to indicate that it was primarily to their shops that the customer would have gone for what is now customarily called 'haberdashery', for it is here, as I have indicated, that one finds the stock of ribbons and points and pins and scissors, garters, hose, silks and knick-knacks which are comprehended in that term. By contrast all the haberdashers' inventories which I have seen from the Oxford area (save one, and he is from the sixteenth century), seem to show that they stuck pretty rigidly to hats. Francis Field, for example, whose inventory was taken in April 1635[27] had fifteen different prices of hat in about five styles, and the rest of the goods listed as in the shop were materials or equipment for moulding, blocking or remaking them. At the end of the century, in 1694, the shop of Thomas Trapp[28] (in a building which also housed a school room) contained hats – if we differentiate by price and colour – of 33 varieties, caps, casters, carolinas, felt hats, and fine hats for women amongst them, but none of the small goods which later came to be associated with the term 'haberdashery'.

Such inventories of petty chapmen as I have seen show that they were mini-mercers, if I may use that term. They had very little of any one thing, but often a surprising variety of things. Richard Kent[29] of Great Faringdon in 1604, for example, had small wares to the value of just over £11, but within this there were: black, brown and white thread and Coventry blue thread, inkle, ordinary gartering, silk gartering, and Welsh gartering, points, laces, pins, soap, brown paper, starch, raisins, aquavita, bone lace, buttons, prunes, currants, sugar, mace, pepper, wormseed, nutmegs, cinnamon, sugar candy, cloves, ginger, and what the appraisers, loath to go into further detail called 'other smawle implementes'. I greatly look forward to seeing the work which Margaret Spufford has been doing on chapmen and their inventories because I am certain that chapmen were key people in the circulation not only of goods, but of news, information, fashion and other intangibles.

Clarke's inventory will serve as an example to show that a mercer's stock overlapped many of the specialist trades: ironmongers and cutlers and apothecaries amongst them. It is evident from Anthony Wood's diary that it was not customary (for him at any rate) to pay cash on the nail at the mercer's. He generally had his goods on tick. The size of the debt books noted in many mercers' inventories reflects this, and as the trading demarcations broke down in the course of the seventeenth century, and the supply of cloth and the making of clothing became united in the same hands, members of the drapery and tailoring trade became credit financiers to generations of Oxford men. The link between undergraduate debt and the clothing trade in Oxford would make an interesting study. Certainly the Chancellor's court was almost wholly a court of debt from the 1660's onwards, and the records of that court provide splendid evidence of retailing practice from the seventeenth to the nineteenth centuries, because of the survival of the copies of the bills put into the court when the recovery of a debt to a tradesman was sought.

It will not be possible, nor perhaps profitable, to speak of many kinds of shop in detail in the space of this short paper. I will limit myself to two other aspects. I will look firstly at one sort of service establishment: the barber's shop. Secondly, I will touch again on the point about the book trade being bolstered financially by that of food and drink.

The barbers were an interesting group in Oxford. Their gild was a University one which, having received a new charter from the Vice-Chancellor in 1675, lasted until 1859.[30] If we contrast the inventories of two barbers – one from the first quarter of the seventeenth century and one from the same quarter of the eighteenth century – we can see documented the change in the barber's role. The shop of William Rixon[31] in May 1623 had three chairs, each with a looking glass, a pair of curling irons, candlestick, basin and hatbrush to it. There was a supply of other basins, bottles, shop cloths etc, and then:

> 'Five cases of toles furnisshed with barbar's instruments' and
> 'Other toles and instruments for drawing of teeth and to let blood, being 12 in number.'

Here, then, was a shop fitted out not only for the care of hair and wigs, but also for primitive dentistry and surgery. It is also interesting to note in this, as in other barbers' inventories of this date, that the shop contained musical instruments. Here there was a viol and a cithern. These were for the use of customers waiting for a trim, perhaps, or with raging toothache, and are an early example of the association between barber shops and music which subsequently flowered elsewhere in the barbershop quartet, and is now mass-produced as canned music to accompany twentieth-century hair stylists. Debts due to Rixon, all secured, amounted to £41. The shop of Thomas Sedgeley,[32] a barber who died in 1714, contrasts with this. In this shop the chairs are of leather and there are almanacs on the walls. Drawers and cupboards line the room and all the equipment is for hair-trimming and for making, washing, curling and re-shaping periwigs. The impression gained (and it may of course be a false one) is that whereas Rixon was part of the world of health and hygiene, Sedgeley's world is that of fashion. This may also account for the fact that money owed to him in his shop book, and apparently unsecured, amounted to over £150 in a total value of £367.

I would now like to turn briefly and finally to the connection between the making and selling of books in Oxford in the seventeenth century and the purveying of food and drink. This is a subject, as I said earlier, which needs a detailed examination, and enough clues survive amongst the papers about which I have been speaking to indicate that such an examination would reveal a good deal about the nature of the financing of the trade. It is well known, for instance that Joseph Barnes, the first university printer, and a bookseller, set up his press in the 1580's at a corner house in the High Street. It is also to be noted that the house was a tavern, and possibly an inn as well. Barnes, who retired in 1617, was a successful printer but had never made it pay. The licence to sell wine which he had had for at least nine years before becoming university printer was allowed to pass to his widow because of their lack of funds. One of his successors as a university printer from 1624 to 1640 was William Turner, again a bookseller before he took over the press. In 1627 he also took over the university licence to sell wine which had passed from Barnes to his widow, and Turner occupied the same tavern. Turner, unlike Barnes, was *not* a success as a printer. Archbishop Laud, appalled at his shoddy and unscholarly work, wanted to dismiss him 'as his extraordinarie peevishnes, or extreme sottishnes (harde to say which) hath deserved'.[33] But he remained printer until his death in the 1640's. What is interesting is that in his probate inventory[34] exhibited in November 1645 he is called not 'bookseller' or 'printer' (by which titles the bibliographers now know him) but 'vintner'; and the tavern or inn, containing rooms with exotic names such as the Lion, the Troy, the Fleur de Lys, the Content, the Maidenhead, the Phoenix, and the Castle, is scheduled in full. True, there was a printhouse and shop there, but no press or type was valued (there may have been good reason for this, of course), and apart from the fittings, the room contained only ten reams of waste paper and 'A parcell of books in quires which will sell for wast paper' and which were valued at £5. Others, too, such as Thomas Pembroke the bookbinder who died in 1673 were innkeepers and directly involved in the food and drink business. But the involvement of others was less obvious. One of the cases in the Chancellor's court in which I have become interested (because it left amongst the papers of the court an inventory of a bookseller's shop in 1687) is that in which a bookseller called Anthony Stephens who had entered the world of publishing and overstretched himself financially, went bankrupt.[35] What I find interesting here is that the four people who sued for the recovery, from Stephens's stock, of money which he had borrowed from them upon bond were Benjamin Cutler, the butler of New College; Nathaniel New, a Holywell innkeeper; George Thomson, the manciple of All Souls' College; and George Edwards, the manciple of New Inn Hall. This George Edwards was also engaged more directly in the book business for, apart from having lent Stephens the money to print 700 copies of the *Elements of Euclid Explain'd,* he was himself a 'cutter of great letters' and an engraver for the university press, and he was the man who, with Bishop Fell's encouragement, set up a paper-mill at Wolvercote, which is still there. Stephens, then, who had not himself diversified into other trades, had had to go to the wealth of the provisions business in order to keep his ship afloat for a while. But he was a bad manager, and in the end it had still foundered.

This has been a somewhat undisciplined paper, touching on a variety of aspects of my subject, and often straying from the point. It only, of course, skates over the surface of a subject which is all the larger because it deals with a small geographical area. This is, as we all know, one of the paradoxes into which one is led if one is what Harry Bell called 'a document snob'. I will accept the criticism of it that much of the mixture is only half digested, but I would defend myself against the charge that the ideas which form the ingredients are only half baked.

Notes

1   Unpublished lecture in the possession of Mrs. E.M. Bell, and quoted with her permission.
2   Dorothy Davis, *A history of shopping* (London, 1966), 149.
3   A. Clark, *The life and times of Anthony Wood . . .,* I–V, Oxford Historical Society, XIX (1891), XXI (1892), XXVI (1894), XXX (1895), XL (1900).
4   John S. Moore, *The goods and chattels of our forefathers: Frampton Cotterell and district probate inventories 1539–1804* (London and Chichester, 1976).

5 J.M. Bestall and D.V. Fowkes, *Chesterfield wills and inventories 1521–1603*, Derbyshire Record Society, I (1977).

6 In *Medical History*, II, (1958), 134–6

7 T.S. Willan, *The Inland trade* (Manchester, 1976).

8 Bodl. Lib. MS. Wills Berks. 98/170

9 D.G. Vaisey, *Probate inventories of Lichfield and district 1568–1680*, Staffordshire Record Society, 4th ser., V (1969), 155–61.

10 In the Lichfield Joint Record Office, Public Library, Lichfield. I am most grateful to Jane Hampartumian for pointing this inventory out to me.

11 John Bartlett, 1675. Bodl. Lib. MS. Wills Berks. 46/118.

12 Margaret Cash, *Devon inventories of the sixteenth and seventeenth centuries*, Devon & Cornwall Record Society, n.s., XI (1966), 169–70

13 His probate documents are Bodl. Lib. MS. Wills Oxon. 149/2/3.

14 D.G. Vaisey, op. cit., 4.

15 His probate documents are Bodl. Lib. MS. Wills Peculiars 51/2/48.

16 *Volpone* Act V, Scenes II and III.

17 Clare St Q. Gittings, 'Funerals in England 1580–1640: the evidence of probate accounts'. Oxford M. Litt. thesis 1978. A copy is in Bodl. Lib. MS M.Litt. d.1890.

18 Oxford University Archives, Chancellor's Court Inventories, Vol. A–Bo, Hyp. B.10.

19 Oxford University Archives, Chancellor's Court Accounts, Vol. A–H, Hyp, B.8.

20 Oxford University Archives, Chancellor's Court Wills, Vol. C, Hyp. B.23; Inventories, Vol. Br–C, Hyp. B.11; Accounts, Vol. A–H, Hyp. B.8; and Registrum Curie Cancellarii 1633–6, Hyp. A.37.

21 Bodl. Lib. MS. Wills Oxon. 171/2/5.

22 D.G. Vaisey and F. Celoria, 'Inventory of George Ecton, 'potter', of Abingdon, Berks, 1696', *Journal of Ceramic History*, 7 (1974), 13–42.

23 Bodl. Lib. MS. Wills Oxon. 164/4/3.

24 Bodl. Lib. MS. Wills Oxon. 171/3/22

25 See n.11 above.

26 Bodl. Lib. MS. Wills Oxon. 11/4/7

27 Bodl. Lib. MS. Wills Oxon. 297/2/1

28 Bodl. Lib. MS. Wills Oxon. 67/2/31.

29 Bodl. Lib. MS. Wills Peculiars 75/4/13

30 J.L. Bolton, 'The Barbers' Company. A University gild', *Oxoniensia*, xxviii (1963), 84–6.

31 Oxford University Archives, Chancellor's Court Inventories, Vol. R–S, Hyp. B.18

32 Ibid.

33 John Johnson and Strickland Gibson, *Print and privilege at Oxford to the year 1700*, Oxford Bibliographical Society, vii (1946), Ch.1.

34 Oxford University Archives, Chancellor's Court Inventories, Vol. T–Y, Hyp. B.19.

35 For Stephens and his shop see D. G. Vaisey, 'Anthony Stephens: the rise and fall of an Oxford bookseller' in *Studies in the book trade in honour of Graham Pollard*, Oxford Bibliographical Society, xviii (1975).

Index